Julie,

Thank you for your support

GRADUATE

Moving from Failure in the Hood to Success Commencement and Beyond

Take care and God bless

Royce Kinniebrew, M.Ed.

The Student Mechanic

Royce K

ISBN: 978-0-692-91934-7

Published by Royce Kinniebrew
royce@therdkgroup.com
www.therdkgroup.com

Photography by China Moore
leomoore08@gmail.com

Printed in the United States of America
First Edition 2017

Dedication

This book is dedicated to Grace for making me aware that I had a story and to Gramps for praying to make sure that I would even have one.

TABLE OF CONTENTS

Dedication ______ *3*

Preface ______ *6*

Chapter 1: JOYCE ELAINE, MY MOM ______ *8*

Chapter 2: Dan Charles, My Dad ______ *14*

Chapter 3: LEE BIVENS, BIB ______ *19*

Chapter 4: STEPHEN ANTHONY, MY BROTHER ______ *23*

Chapter 5: RUTH ALBERTA, GRAMPS, MY GRANDMOTHER ______ *29*

Chapter 6: FAMILY MATTERS ______ *34*

Chapter 7: ROHNS STREET ______ *36*

Chapter 8: BULLIES R US ______ *48*

Chapter 9: THE WONDER YEARS ______ *50*

Chapter 10: THOSE CASS TECHNICIANS ______ *54*

Chapter 11: WELCOME TO THE JUNGLE, KETTERING HIGH SCHOOL ______ *58*

Chapter 12: TERI THE FIRST "LOVE" ______ *70*

Chapter 13: BURGE RESIDENCE HALL ______ *75*

Chapter 14: THE AWAKENING ______ *82*

Chapter 15: G.K., LAMES LEE, AND THE AFRO HOUSE ______ *88*

Chapter 16: BLACK HAWK DOWN ______ *92*

Chapter 17: GRADUATION TIME 102

Chapter 18: THE W(RIGHT) MUSEUM 107

Chapter 19: JUMPING THE POND 116

Chapter 20: HOUSE OF HORRORS 122

Chapter 21: THE GRIOT PROGRAM, M.ED. 125

Chapter 22: THE TAB 129

Chapter 23: BROTHER IN BEIJING 137

Chapter 24: FEAR AND LOATHING IN BRAZIL 141

Chapter 25: MARSHALL, U OF D, DPA, AND THE STUDENT MECHANIC 152

Chapter 26: CONCLUSION, THE CLIFF NOTES 158

Resources 162

Preface

As a public speaker and educator, I have visited many wonderful places around the world. Brazil, China, Puerto Rico, Canada, and the UK are several of the international locations. London, England was the first place I needed to use my passport. (Canada doesn't count. When I was young, before 9/11, we would pile up in a friend's pickup and drive to Windsor, Ontario where the drinking age was 18 with no problem.) I have met a number of great people as well. My friends in the UK are especially important. One inspired me to write this book.

Grace Ononiwu gave me the idea. She is a highly successful legal mind in England. "Royce, you need to write your story" she said with that unmistakable British accent. "I have a story?" I thought. At that time, I believed people with a story were soldiers, or professional athletes, entertainers, or someone who had overcame some life-threatening illness. I was neither.

After thinking about it, I realized Grace was right. Maybe I hadn't done something to have my face plastered across CNN, Sports Center, or C-Span. Yet, I had traveled the world, lectured to thousands, earned a master's degree, and lifted myself out of the dangerous ghetto of Detroit, Michigan. My rags to riches route through education and life is a testament of perseverance and self-discipline.

Dropping out of high school in some places is more the norm than the exception. The Detroit Public Schools flirt with having the highest dropout rate in the nation. Not completing college is just as problematic.

Only about 40% of African-Americans graduate from college in 6 years or less. My story shows how both can be done in the face of great adversity.

After college, I continued to use the same strategies and behaviors that led to my success. They were universal. Whenever present, they lead to success. Whenever absent failure was certain. It was that simple.

This book is not an exhaustive autobiography of everything I have done, the people I have met, or my accomplishments. It is a collection of life events that relate directly to completing high school, college, and how I became successful in my professional life.

Mine is a part cautionary tale and part inspirational message. Closely looking back on my life, I realize that I indeed had a story. Now knowing the data on high school dropouts, incarceration rates of young black males, and statistics on teenage pregnancy (as well as other social ills) I realized that my life made the screeching tires sound many times, but never the fatal accident. The most important factor was the skill, hard work, and determination of me, the driver.

Chapter 1
JOYCE ELAINE, MY MOM

All that I am, or I hope to be, I owe to my angel mother – Abraham Lincoln

My mom was groovy, cool, and hip all at the same time. She was stylish, wore curly afro wigs, and would be seen dressed in the finest clothes of the 60's and 70's. Can you imagine Beyoncé in bell bottoms? That was my mom. If she were a car, my mom would have been a convertible Cadillac Eldorado.

Children are a reflection of their parents. That was my brother and I. My mom dressed us in nice clothes. I can remember shopping at J.L. Hudson's, now Macy's. We wore Sassoon jeans. They were the True Religion jeans of the 70's. My mom kept us in the newest fashions.

Garanimals were the fancy too. They were tops and bottoms with different animals on them. Started in 1972, this company lauded the fact that a child could pick their own clothes by matching the animals on shirts and pants thus creating a sense of independence and self-confidence. I wonder why it didn't work for me. Kids would sometimes try and make fun of my colorful matching outfits, but they found it difficult because everyone knew it was expensive stuff.

Joyce Elaine Kinniebrew would take trips. Usually, she would head down to that destination of all cool people: Las Vegas. Dean Martin, Sammy Davis Jr., Frank Sinatra, and Elvis knew that if you wanted to have a good time, come to Vegas. She did. Towing a group of her cool friends, she set out to Sin City often. She would always bring us back some of those awful souvenirs because she loved us.

On other occasions, my mom would head north of the border. She would go to the annual Caribana Festival that usually occurred the first weekend in August. Toronto, Ontario was a short 4 hour drive from Detroit. Twenty years later, her "cool" son would follow her footsteps to experience the Caribbean-inspired festivities. It's now called the Scotiabank Caribbean Carnival. My brother and I loved our local trips with my mother too.

We would go to the Belair, Gratiot, or the Ford-Wyoming Drive-Ins. The latter is the only one to survive the wrecking ball. We loved these excursions. Usually, there was a playground near the screen where kids of all productions dates, makes, and models would play. Concession food, hanging with our mom, and a playground full of kids was big fun for the folks from Rohns Street. This was Heaven. We enjoyed ourselves way too much on one visit.

They would usually play two movies twice. In case you missed the beginning of one, you could stay around for the second nightly showing. We did this one night and dozed off. Knock, Knock, Knock we heard on the window of our Chevy Impala. It was broad daylight. We had slept all night. I guess the drive-in employee that woke us up had too. He looked as drowsy and confused as we did. We laughed all the way home. Soon life would be no laughing matter.

My mother went crazy. Not in the sense that she is hard to deal with, or mean, or hilarious at dinner parties, but in the literal sense. Her mental illness was real. We have no idea what caused my mother's paranoid episodes. They started with no warning, no introduction, and no user manual. She often made claims that people were harming her, my brother, or I. None were the case.

Her illness came on the scene when I was about 9 or 10 years old. It never left. It has haunted her since then with varying intensity. One day she could be the witty, calm, and cool mom I remembered. The next day she would be accusing people of the most outlandish, foolhardy, and bizarre things. It was like hitting the gas when you should be pumping the brakes. She would be out of control.

My mother's condition was hard for me to understand. It was hard for us to understand. She had not fallen down a flight of stairs, been hit by a car, or experienced some other outward sign of physical trauma. She was not a crack addict. That would have been easier to deal with and understand. She was troubled on the inside where we couldn't see. Almost overnight, she had become a stranger.

Our extended family was made up of my mother, brother, myself, grandmother, and grandfather. He was not my real grandfather, but my grandmother's significant other. On occasion, my mother would accuse him of hurting her. There was no proof, only accusations. It made no sense. It took most of my adult life to realize that it wasn't supposed to.

My mom said that she was shot in the back by my granddad. This was her main delusion. We wondered where these claims came from. We looked for an injury, blood, or something to show her that this wasn't so. Our problem was trying to reason with someone unreasonable. Black people don't usually handle mental illness properly. We tried to be logical when there was no logic present. We looked at an empty gas gauge, the light blinking, and wondered why the car wouldn't move.

She even claimed that my grandfather sexually abused me. That claim was accompanied with a physical examination that was confusing, uncomfortable, and embarrassing. My young mind could not process what was happening. No one ever abused me.

This examination occurred in her room behind The Door. She would go in her bedroom, then close, and barricade the door with a dresser. It was like a scene from a horror movie. I slept in that room for months. The fear she had was real. It just was imaginary. It didn't exist. Just as troubling was the violence.

My grandmother was old school. She didn't like people lying, stealing, or cheating. She especially didn't like her daughter accusing her man of hurting me. They would fight. On numerous occasions my grandmother and mother got into knockdown drag-out fist fights. My grandfather and brother would have to separate them. It got so bad that they would break furniture. Imagine the two most important women in the world rolling on the floor cussing and fighting. It's hard for me to think of, even today.

After one such brawl, we moved out. We ventured way next door. Some of our relatives lived beside us in a two-family flat. The upstairs was empty. That's where my mother, brother, and I parked ourselves for months. It was like going from the frying pan into the fire. It was depressing.

GRADUATE

The electricity was not on at the new place. We stayed there anyway. It must have been 2 or 3 weeks before the lights were turned on. Those mark some of my darkest days figuratively and literally. The blackness pierced me like a hunter's arrow. I felt like I died a million times in that dark house. Fear was my only friend. I was not yet 12 years old.

I was not usually that afraid of the dark. But, there I was. I suppose the inability to turn on the lights made me fear the piercing blackness even more. It amplified it, made it more foreboding, more inescapable. I was trapped in the shadows.

My grandparents were normal. They had served as a buffer for my mother's craziness. Even though they were no more than 20 feet away, their influence was gone. I felt alone in the house with 2 other people. Everything that was familiar to me was upside down. I was upside down. What a terrible way to live.

My brother had been invited to church with some of his band member friends from Martin Luther King high school. He liked it. He loved it. It probably seemed normal to a kid from an abnormal home life. It was his escape. I wished it were mine.

One day my brother wanted to go to an event at the church. My mother didn't want him to go. She made some paranoid claim about what was going on. She said that he was in danger there. To her everyone was in danger everywhere. Of course that was not so. This was the tipping point for my brother. He was fed up.

Stephen was about 15 or 16 years old. He was much stronger than my mother. When she tried to stop him by beating him with a broom, he pushed past her with ease. She couldn't physically stop him. He rumbled down the stairs and was gone. There I stood shocked. There I stood afraid. There I stood alone.

I was not afraid that my mother would hurt me. She never physically did that. Her illness would isolate me; it put me in solitary confinement. I was separated from those who could love me properly: my brother, grandfather, and grandmother.

One night when I was laying in the bed, I thought I saw something in the corner of the ceiling. All the lights were turned off. It was darker than the darkness. It moved. Seemingly, it slithered like a snake in the corners of my room. The terror I felt was real. I would have several more nights like that.

Abraham Lincoln said, "All that I am or ever hope to be, I owe to my angel mother." He was right.

In that dark of darkness, I was not consumed. I was not destroyed. I neither lost my mind, my way, or my will to live. The sickness that gripped my mother did not become my own. It was not able to lay its foul hands on my innocent little soul.

This was not my doing. My strength alone was not able to bear it. I attribute my salvation on the prayers, love, and guidance of one woman. My grandmother, Ruth Alberta, was an angel indeed. She saved me.

Chapter 2

Dan Charles, My Dad

A father is a man who expects his son to be as good a man as he meant to be – Frank A. Clark

My brother, Stephen, told me that once when he was visiting our father that he had flirted with some haggardly women barely fit to haunt a house. That was our dad. He was a deacon on one hand and heathen on the other. Aren't we all? By the end of his life, he was mostly the deacon.

A boy should have the presence of his father. I don't know this because of experience. It is something I have learned through observation, study, and hardship. When life presented the age old questions of love, responsibility, and integrity, I failed miserably. I had to learn about manhood the hard way: on the mean streets of Detroit and the corn fields of Iowa. The school of hard knocks found me to be a poor student.

Dan Charles Green was my father. He died of complications from diabetes and high blood pressure. We weren't close. We didn't have much of a relationship. It hurts me to write this, but it is true. For some reason, he was a much better uncle than father. I'm not alone in this daddy dilemma.

My father had five children (that we know of) by three women. He didn't bother to marry any of his children's mothers. I have a brother, a half-sister, and two half-brothers (one is deceased). The halves are wholes now. I love all my brothers and sister dearly. His relationship with them is similar to his relationship with me: limited.

Did he love us? Yes, I'm sure he did. Did he know how to show it? No, I'm sure he didn't. That I believe he may have learned from his father. When we were younger, elementary school age, he was somewhat present in my life. He would come and visit. We would visit him. My father never lived with us. I would however find out years later that my brother Stephen lived with him on several occasions. Sometimes my brother Stephen and I would ride the bikes that our dad gave us to visit him. That was a joy.

My dad made bikes. He didn't forge the steel, but he did assemble the parts. How he got all those parts, I don't know. His house looked like a bicycle repair shop. There were usually several bikes somewhere along the assembly process sitting around his house. Some missing a tire, seat, handle bars, and some just bare frames. It was a manly kind of place.

He made me a five-speed that invoked envy in my friends. It had to be something from the 50's or 60's, but it wasn't shabby. It had a thicker back tire like a motorcycle. The gear shift box was down on the frame. The lever looked like one you would find in a car. It was sweet indeed. That bike was more for cruising than for stunts. I would find that out after the handle bars gave way during one of my landings from a homemade Evel Knievel style ramp. I hurt my ego as well as my man package.

The other joys were trips to Cedar Point amusement park in Sandusky, Ohio. For some reason, I don't remember my father ever attending. But, I'm sure he did. My aunt Ann, my dad's sister, arranged the trips. She would charter a nice bus. People from the family church, associates, and friends made up the passengers. I was really young. I couldn't have been more than 7 or 8 years old. My brother and I were put in her care. We never got lost, missed a meal, or longed for anything while we were away on those day trips. These are some of the best memories of my childhood. I felt like I belonged.

Visiting my dad was fun. He was the perennial bachelor. His mindset was different. We had more room to be boys. There were no mamas or grand mammas wiping the corners of our mouths, telling us to pull up our pants, or to finish our vegetables. My dad had a pellet gun that he would allow my brother and I to play with, unsupervised. In today's timeout, cotton candy parenting world that would have led to a call to child protective services.

My dad kept a loaded gun sitting in plain view as well. It was a 9 mm German Lugar. I'll never forget it. Depending on when we came over to visit, it would be sitting on the toilet, dining room table, or in the kitchen somewhere. My father simply said, "Don't touch it." We never did. It was understood. We marveled at it as closely as one could get without touching. I shudder to think of such a thing from today's viewpoint and my M. Ed. adult mind.

My paternal grandmother lived on the ground floor of a two-family home. My dad lived in the flat over her. I was too young to appreciate Sarah Green. She had a skin disorder that caused her skin to turn white. As a youngster, I thought that this was yucky. She passed away when I was in my early 30s. I cried like a baby when she did. She was one of the kindest, sweetest, and loving people I have ever met. I never heard a mean thing come out of her mouth. I would love to give her a kiss on one of those milky cheeks right now if I could.

My father was a drag racer in the car. I remember his driving to be exhilarating. As an adult, I would call it reckless. He would speed down residential streets at dizzying speed. When he was younger his driving license would be in some state of restriction. He would get his act together and become the driver for his church. Just like all people, my father evolved into a better version of himself. Unfortunately, I didn't have the pleasure of experiencing that change when I think I needed it.

As we got older, we stopped visiting as much. Maybe our developing sense of right and wrong made us uncomfortable to be around him. I'm not sure. By the time my brother got married when I was 14, I barely saw my father. That was about the same time my mother's mental illness started to set in. From that point, I was destined to wander. My father had showed me precisely how it was done. He made countless bad decisions that I witnessed. The supreme one was how to raise your children.

I learned that his father was a tough man, even mean. Growing up in the South at the turn of the century surely could do that to a Black man. It shed much light on to my father's behavior. I understood that everyone could have a crappy childhood. I understood how that could impact adulthood. Years of failure would pass for me before I made peace with my dad.

My siblings, Debra, Burnest, Stephen, and I, stood hands clasped, heads bowed, with watery eyes. Our dad's retirement home had now become a hospice. Each of us took turns praying for my dying father. He laid there on the bed- a shell of his former self. Dan Green had become frail, partially blind, and unable to walk. His body was shutting down right before us. We were all successful adults with families and careers. We realized that we were not defined by our father's mistakes. We were defined by our own successes and failures. So in that moment, we understood. We forgave him for his absenteeism. As my brother Stephen was concluding the last prayer of forgiveness, reconciliation, and love, our father died. Hopefully, he rode to heaven on our love and prayers.

Chapter 3
LEE BIVENS, BIB

There are fathers who do not love their children; there is no grandfather who does not adore his grandson. – Victor Hugo

Lee Bivens, or Bib as we called him, was much different than my father. He was more dependable, sensible, more like the dad from the Fresh Prince of Bel Air TV program. In essence, he was my Grandmother's boyfriend. We looked at him as though he was our grandfather. He took on that responsibility without reservation. My paternal and maternal grandfathers were both dead before I could remember. Bib was the best thing- and the only thing- I had in that position. He was a good man.

I don't know how he and my Grandmother met, but from my earliest memories as a child, he was there. Grandfather was a role made for him. He was kind, light-hearted, and dutiful. I never heard arguments about money, bills, or a hot plate of food on the table in our house growing up. He left for work every day at Budd Wheels, an auto supplier. He would say, "I'll see you in the cool of the evening." That was his catchphrase.

GRADUATE

Bib gave my mother the first car I remember her owning. I don't know the terms. Things like that were far above my pay-grade as a child. I just know we owned 2 cars in the 70's like virtually everyone else on the block. We were a middle-class extended family.

Bib and Gramps would take Sunday drives. They were so fun. I was allowed to tag along in the back seat with my brother and mom. Sunday cruising was straight out of another time. It paid respect to the fact that Black people didn't always have cars. It was like saying "we made it this far in spite of."

I saw parts of the Detroit area that many kids did not. The Vernors plant on Woodward, the big stove on Jefferson as you drove on to Belle Isle, and the huge homes of Indian Village with their manicured lawns and carriage houses big enough to live in. They were fantastic to a kid in elementary school. Bib loved us and we loved him. Things would change though, as they always do.

No one worked out. My Mother, Grandmother, nor Bib ever lifted a finger to stay in shape. We ate whatever we wanted to. Some of Gramp's dishes were delicious, but very unhealthy. Her pot roast and potatoes were scrumptious. After being refrigerated, the meat and potatoes would be stuck in the hardened juices which were mostly fat. Whose body could hold up to that type of diet?

During my junior year in high school, Bib had a massive stroke that left him unable to work. One side of his body drooped from the debilitating medical episode. He slurred his words too. It was awful. The kindest man I knew was under attack from the inside. This marked the end to a life of more than enough; and introduced me to hardly enough.

My grandmother and Bib were not married. That was the first problem. His daughter was the second. Seemingly, she had an axe to grind. My grandmother knew nothing of common law marriage and lawyers. They had been living together for 20 years by the time he had the stroke. Gramps sat by and watched her life take a drastic turn without doing anything about it.

Bib's daughter got power of attorney over his estate. She immediately moved him out. Since he was the main breadwinner- we were in huge financial trouble really quickly. We were unable to pay the mortgage, property taxes, or monthly bills. My mother had not worked in years- suffering from mental illness. The disability checks Gramps received were a mere drop in the bucket. My brother was struggling to stay afloat himself having just started his own family. The road we were on was a dead end.

In the course of a few months all our utilities were turned off. We were living with no electricity, phone, or water. We only had gas service. I remember having to go next door to fill up a pot of water from my relative's water hose. I would take that pot of water and heat it up on the stove. That's how I would bath.

I would try to get out to that hose early enough so that no one would see me. I'd wait a few moments after someone walked by and dash up the front stairs with my bathtub in hand. The shame and embarrassment of living like that was bewildering. I thank God this didn't last forever, trouble never does. There is always some relief to life's difficulties. There is always light at the end of the tunnel.

We got on welfare, received food stamps, and donations from the Focus Hope pantry of canned goods. After a few months, I could stop bathing out of pots. All the utilities would be turned back on. We were able to survive. The Sunday drives were over but at least we could eat.

GRADUATE

Life was different. There were no more designer clothes for me. They came from the second hand store. The drive-in was out because we no longer owned a car. My mother didn't take any more trips. These were the lean years. We held on to the most important thing we had: each other.

Bib would come over and visit us from time to time. All though he did not go back to work, he had made almost a full recovery. He was able to speak and walk without any detection of his previous medical condition. That made me really happy.

I talked to him about getting back power of attorney over his affairs. He never did. He seemed broken and unsure of himself. Dependency had set in like a coma. He would never be the same. His body was able, but his mind was not. Fear had kept him from changing his situation. Like it always does; it tries to keep you from living life to the fullest.

His daughter moved him to the basement of her house where her son once stayed. That is the last I heard of Bib for many years. I was out of college when I heard in passing that he had died. My heart sunk. I wished I could have seen him before he died. How I loved that man whose potbelly was a pillow for my woolly little head on many occasions.

Chapter 4

STEPHEN ANTHONY, MY BROTHER

I don't believe an accident of birth makes people sisters or brothers. It makes them siblings, gives them mutuality of parentage. Sisterhood and brotherhood is a condition people have to work at. – Maya Angelou

My brother was my hero. I owe so much of who I am to him. He had to shoulder the wind of being the big brother. That is hard. Big brothers and big sisters are like those armored vehicles with the battering ram on the front that the police and military use. They make a way for others to come up behind them. Stephen did that for me in many ways. We had so much fun growing up.

I had a potty mouth growing up. Actually it was more like an open sewer. I could cuss the buttons off of a sailor's uniform. I would do this at my brother's command. He was the organ grinder and I was the monkey. We were a team.

I can remember going to the 4-H Club, a recreational center about 5 or 6 blocks from our house. He gave the sign and I commenced with a filth-laden rant of swear words that sent the other children into a frenzy. I was no older than 6 years old.

Bigger kids' eyes bulged in amazement as to say, "Where can I get one of those?"

We had a dog named Spot growing up. My mother told me the story of how he blocked me from running into the street when I was a toddler. We gave him these dog biscuits to eat. They looked like cookies. Naturally, I ate them on occasion. My brother thought this was funny then. I do now.

Stephen had a serious crush on a girl across the street. He was smitten. She was the apple of his eye. We didn't live in a convent. There was always a bottle of some alcohol around. My mom was a Bacardi type of girl. We were forbidden to touch the stuff, until this one day. My brother was about 14 or 15. Someway my brother conned my mom into letting him have a taste. He drank the whole bottle in one continuous gulp. We were all shocked. Needless to say he was drunk in 15 minutes.

My mom wouldn't let him go outside. He was forced to stay inside. That didn't matter. He was at the screen door professing his love to the girl across the street. It was in the middle of the day. It was high comedy 101. You could hear the other neighbors laughing at Dark Gable. He finished the day off with a forwards front flip on his bed that put a hole in the wall with his foot. He slept well that night.

My brother had swollen due to the unhealthy, yet delicious meals served in our house. He was going through his chunky stage in high school. I don't know what started his fitness interest. Joining the marching band at Kettering high school may have had something to do with it. Whatever the case, he was obsessed. He got a weight set and started to go running at night.

He worked his way up to running probably 4 or 5 miles, maybe more. He was committed to it. It was his passion. His weight dropped pretty fast. He had transformed himself from a doughboy into a muscle head in no time. During high school after Stephen got married and moved out, I would run those same routes alone as we did 5 years earlier.

I would go out with him sometimes on my bike and rode next to him while he ran. Imagine riding your bike through the streets of Detroit at night at the age of 11 or 12. I was living the adolescent life. You couldn't beat this fun with a stick. My brother was even more committed to his music.

I think my brother was a prodigy. He took to the trumpet like a bird to flight. It was connected to him like an arm or leg. He practiced continuously. I would be riding my bike blocks away and hear him practicing. He was the first example I saw of a person throwing their whole self into something. It was Divine.

My brother took lessons from a local jazz musician named Marcus Belgrave. He was a living legend. By the time my brother met him, he had worked with Ray Charles, Ella Fitzgerald, Dizzy Gillespie, Sammy Davis Jr., and Tony Bennett just to name a few. He saw something great in Stephen.

Once he took my brother to play a set with him. I tagged along. There I was, barely in middle school hanging out with a jazz legend and my hero. My brother played with the band into the wee hours of the night. It was long after midnight when we returned home. On the drums that night was a guy named Max Roach. It would take me a long time to appreciate the cool factor of that evening.

At that same period in his life, my brother was getting in touch with his faith, his spirituality. We had always had God on the radar in our house, but now he was becoming center stage for my brother. When he transferred from Kettering to King high school, his friends in the Jazz band helped this happen. They did something very simple. The invited him to church. That one action changed the entire Kinniebrew household.

As usual, I was hanging on my brother's coattails to his new hangout spot: church. I would go to choir rehearsal with him and sit out in the pews and watch. Until one day a woman said, "Since Royce is always here, he can come up here and sing with us." There I was singing in the adult choir. I've been singing ever since.

My brother would soon invite my Grandmother to church. She came with no reservations. We were church people who didn't regularly go to service. Gramps would become a part of the church Mothers. They were a group of women who gave their wisdom to a body of people who desperately needed it. It was a role fit for my grandmother. She had seen a lot and life had taught her well.

One of the dearest pictures of my childhood is one of my grandmothers with her sisters in faith- dressed in all white. It looks like they were dressed for Heaven itself. They sat on pews in the church sanctuary smiling politely wearing their fashionable church hats. That picture resides on my church's wall even today.

My brother even invited my mother to church. He had moved back in from a short stay with my father. She declined. She never set one foot in that church, not even for her mother's funeral. That baffled me. It showed me though how consuming mental illness can be.

My brother graduated from high school and his next adventure was college. He attended Calvin College in Grand Rapids, Michigan. It was a Christian college. It wasn't long before I took a trip to see him. I was in awe of this place. It looked like a big playground to me. The first night we had a massive snowball fight which contained at least 20 or 30 kids.

One side made a slingshot out of a tree that hurled snowballs nearly 100 yards.

Calvin College was not the Detroit Public Schools or King high school. It was more difficult. They had higher expectations. All colleges do. My brother wasn't prepared for the academic load. I would have the same issues in Iowa City, Iowa. It wasn't that he couldn't be successful there. I don't think he gave his inner drive the time to kick in.

The problem with dropping out of college is guilt and regret. They can creep up on you like a lion on the African savannah. The pain of academic failure can last a life time. I don't remember ever talking to him about it. I wouldn't have known what to say at the time. Soon I would be busy making a mess of my freshmen year at Cass Tech high school.

My brother and I were having trouble with the same things. We couldn't quite figure out the school thing. Neither of us was dumb. In retrospect, I can see how we were unskilled as students. We didn't know that there was a recipe for success. Up until that point, we really had not been challenged. We were getting good enough grades by just showing up. Those academic grace periods runs out by Halloween in your first year of college. There is only trick or treat.

We started attending another church on the Southwest side of the city. I really don't know why we didn't return to the Tree of Life Missionary Baptist Church. It had been good to us. Many of his friends were still away at college. Maybe facing the questions about college were more than Stephen wanted to handle.

Life back under your parent's roof can be a rude awakening for a person who has experienced the freedom of college. I don't know if that was the case for my brother or not. I couldn't read his mind and have never talked to him about that time in his life. I do know that he met a young woman at this new church. My brother was married within a year. I'll never forget the wedding ceremony.

Right before the wedding service, I ducked out to use the restroom. When I returned, they had gotten started. Even though I was a groomsman, no one missed me. I watched my brother get married from a side doorway. I felt demoralized. It wasn't about me; but I did want to be a part of this important day for my brother. He was my hero after all.

Things would never be the same for my brother and I. The woman he married had a child from a previous relationship, and another one on the way. He would not have time to play jazz music into the night or take long runs with his snotty-nosed brother in tow. He had to provide for his family. I couldn't imagine being 18 with a child and one on the way. That must have been scary. Whatever the case, we drifted apart.

Chapter 5

RUTH ALBERTA, GRAMPS, MY GRANDMOTHER

We should all have one person who knows how to bless us despite the evidence; Grandmother was that person for me – Phyllis Theroux

My grandmother was like the Tale of Two Cities. She could be the best of times and the worst of times. Woe unto you if you had to see the worst part. She was as protective as a mother bear. It would serve you well to leave her cubs alone.

When my brother Stephen, 4 years my elder, got into an altercation, the mother bear came out. Someway my grandmother found out that he was about to get into some deep trouble. The story goes, my grandmother blasted out of the back door of our house like a drag racer at the site of green.

At that time my grandmother was still in her forties. She was still ready to rumble. And that she did. In 70s Detroit, we still had usable alleys. Our garbage dumpsters were located behind our backyards with enough room for enormous trucks to drive thru and scoop them up.

My grandmother was said to "rumble" down the alley like a truck running towards the trouble. She raced to my brother with gravel crunching under her feet with every step. She was focused on getting my brother no matter the cost.

When she got there she pulled my brother out of the jaws of trouble in the nick of time. I don't remember exactly what was going on; but I do know my grandmother wasn't afraid to get into the action. Just leave her cubs alone.

I had decided to go to college out of state. It was a daunting challenge because I didn't know a soul where I was going. Plus, it was 500 miles away. That was 500 miles farther than I had ever been away from home. It would be an adventure like no other up to that point in my life…

When my grandmother was at church, she was asked about where I was. She told them I attended the University of Iowa. The man told my grandmother "that wasn't going to work out." The quick slap across his face said it was. Just leave her cubs alone.

Just as she could lay hand to face, she could lay it to the stove. She was a phenomenal cook. Many dishes she prepared, I have not tasted anything better. Maybe they did not contain her secret ingredient: love.

Most people prepare spaghetti in one of two ways: Sauce on the side or sauce in one big pot with the noodles. My grandmother was the "one big pot" type of lady. I had seen her cook this dish plenty of times and have never been able to duplicate its taste. It was so good a person had to take off their shoes and socks to wiggle their toes in satisfaction as they ate.

Not to be outdone was her cornbread. This was not the Jiffy out of the box type of cornbread. This was made from scratch- cornbread cooked in a big black cast iron skillet. You added your own butter as you liked. On many occasions, I ate the cornbread by itself. It was a meal on its own. My grandmother had to learn how to cook at an early age.

My grandmother gave birth to my mother at the ripe old age of 15. In 1941 this must have been scandalous. Nevertheless, my grandmother made it work. To a large degree my mother and grandmother were like sisters. They grew up together. They lived together practically their entire lives.

I've heard many stories of how my grandmother, as a young girl, had to work in deplorable conditions in a slaughter house. Killing chickens in the Eastern Market district of Detroit put money in her purse and food on the table. Also, it would contribute to my grandmother's debilitating arthritis in her old age.

While I was away at college things started to change for my grandmother. The feisty woman was beginning to mellow with age. She didn't rumble anymore down alleys, she walked with a cane. It was hard for me to see her losing the fight we all must wage against Father Time.

Right before I graduated from college, my grandmother's aging arthritic knees gave out. She took a tumble that she never really recovered from. When I walked in the door and saw her using a walker, my young foolish eyes were barely able to bear it. My champion was getting old and feeble.

Two decades had passed since my mother and grandmother would roll around on the coliseum floor like gladiators. They mellowed together. My mother played the role of dutiful daughter when she wasn't saying or doing something odd. Most of the time, she just seemed eccentric. That's what we wanted to believe at least.

My grandmother had a physical therapist that would visit the house. He would put her through a routine of exercises. She had made a physical recovery from her fall, but not a mental one. For the last 3 or 4 years of her life, she refused to leave the house. No matter what I said, she wouldn't budge. She was stuck in the mud.

This spirit of fear hung over my grandmother. She had given in to it. She stopped challenging it. She stopped pushing back. Her world became smaller and smaller. She allowed fear to suck away her life. I watched it all happen, powerless.

Her trips to the front porch stopped. Then, she left empty her familiar spots around the house where she would read and look at the T.V. Lastly, she just sat and lay in her room. There was nowhere else to go in this world. Time was running out.

One day I came home from work at the museum. My grandmother was unable to speak clearly. I thought it was a natural part of her decline. The next day at work, I realized that my grandmother had suffered a stroke. I dashed home from work and called the ambulance. She was taken to the hospital. She would never see home again.

I visited her the next day. She was unconscious. A breathing tube had been placed in her nose. A trickle of blood marked the spot where the tube rested. I sat at my Grandmother's side and apologized for not being a better grandson. I really don't think that mattered right then. I felt so guilty for something that was out of my control.

It took me a long time to learn and appreciate that life boils down to just a few unmistakable things. One of them is that the relationships with our family, and loved ones, are more important than any material possession. They are the life blood of our existence. Everything else really doesn't matter much.

The following day my next door neighbor called me and said the hospital had called with a message for me. I thought that was strange until I realized that they didn't have a phone number for next of kin. I returned their call.

The doctor's voice was shaky and faint. He told me that when my grandmother had entered the hospital that her heart was very weak. This was the softener, the setup for what he would say next. "Her heart stopped" he whispered. "She died this morning" he said. I was devastated.

When I hung up the phone, I collapsed on my bed in an indescribable fit of tears. It was a mixture of screaming, sobbing, and groaning. It was like an anchor had been placed around my neck and I was being pulled to the bottom of despair. My beating heart had been pulled from my chest. All of this anguish with no Bib, no Stephen, and really no Joyce. My isolation magnified my sadness. I had no one to cry with. I did it all alone.

Two awesome young women who I had been dating carried me through this time of darkness. I don't think they knew how important they were. I was a wreck. They would hold me and wipe my tears like I was a defenseless child. At that moment, I was.

Losing my grandmother helped me to appreciate the importance of family. We don't select them. We don't vote on them. We are placed with them. To deal with them, God gave us patience, intelligence, and wisdom to do so. I don't believe our family members are given to us by accident. I truly believe we are assigned one to another. We are obligated to our family. They need us to be what's best for them. Many times that's not what they want. It is though exactly what they need.

Chapter 6
FAMILY MATTERS

The bond that links your true family is not (just) one of blood, but of respect and joy of each other's life – Richard Bach

Countless times we have heard that family is everything. That is an opinion that I share. The influence of family on a person's life is unmistakable. How many family recipes have been passed down through the years? Skills from the vocations like carpentry, landscaping, and automobile repair have been taught and learned from father to son, Mother to daughter, and parent to child. Lawyers, doctors, firefighters, police officers, and military service people can be seen for generations through generations of particular families.

In a health crisis when a person is in need of a kidney, bone marrow, or blood, relatives are sought first for a match. Families share genetics and have similar DNA. That's why the doctor asks you about your family history. It's important. Your family matters.

But, just like a car, you have been assembled. Hopefully, your family has helped to construct a perseverant, self-disciplined, hard-working, self-confident person with high self-esteem. Those character traits are essential for success. Without them life will be extremely difficult.

Unfortunately, parents make mistakes. Whether by accident or purposefully- mothers and fathers get it wrong. Their children bear the burden. Many have been put together with either faulty parts or faulty workmanship. People that have been hurt are experts at hurting others. This can lead to a life of mediocrity, suffering, and despair, if you let it.

On the assembly line of my early life, I missed some things. I blamed my childhood for my problems for years. But, just like an automobile can be assembled, it can be unassembled and made over. I learned that I was not limited by the shortcomings of my family and childhood. What was necessary for my success was not who I was- but who I was willing to become.

Chapter 7
ROHNS STREET

Yesterday is gone. Tomorrow has not yet come. We have only today. Let us begin. – Mother Teresa

Rohns Street was no different than any other African-American middle-class community in the Midwest. You might see the same type of place in Gary, Indiana, Chicago, Illinois, Cleveland, Ohio, or the like. It was the product of the Great Black Migration and opportunity. For 40 to 50 years at the beginning of the 20th century, Blacks left the South looking for better social and employment opportunities. Many found it in the factories of the North. Five million blacks deposited themselves into Northern Centers. Cities grew rapidly.

The Black population exploded when Henry Ford created the assembly line. In 1914, Ford made a bold move by increasing wages by over 100%. To produce the model-T, "the car that put America on wheels" any able-bodied man was paid $5 dollars a day (Davis & Wagner, 2002, pr.29). This was up to 20 times more than what some African-American sharecroppers were making in the segregated South. Imagine being offered 1 million dollars to leave your 50K job. The pipeline from the fields to the factories had been opened.

Tens of thousands left on trains, in automobiles, and by foot- heading to Detroit. The Black population grew from 5,751 in 1914 to over 145,000 in 1942 (Williams, 2009, pg.7). Residents were mostly crammed into the Black Bottom Neighborhood. Found there was a dark, rich soil that gave the place its name prior to the arrival of Blacks. It was bordered by Gratiot Avenue, Brush Street, Vernor Highway, and the Grand Trunk railroad tracks on Detroit's near Eastside. Segregation kept most African-Americans penned into that area.

Dwight Eisenhower signed the Federal Aid Highway Act in 1956 that would lead to the construction of the Chrysler Freeway. I-75 (and 375) stretches from Michigan to Florida. It led to the demolition of Black Bottom. Paradise Valley, an adjacent entertainment district, would lose prominence as well.

At its height, one could walk over from Black Bottom to Paradise Valley. On the marquee of many night spots could have been Pearl Bailey, Duke Ellington, Ella Fitzgerald, Count Basie, or Sammy Davis Jr. One would frequently see enjoying the district those like politician Adam Clayton Powell, Jesse Owens, and the Brown Bomber, Joe Louis. If remorseful for your prior night's activities, you could go to New Bethel Baptist Church pastured by Aretha Franklins father, C.L. Franklin located right in Paradise Valley on Hastings Street. Black Bottom's demise led to the dispersal of African-Americans into previously segregated areas.

Rohns Street was one of those areas. It is located on the mid Eastside of Detroit. During its heyday, homes were maintained, lawns were manicured, and cars fresh off the assembly line of Chrysler, Ford, or General Motors, sat proudly down both sides of the street. There were no vacant lots and abandoned homes, there was little crime, and it was fully integrated.

Most families had at least one person in the household that worked for the Big Three (Chrysler, Ford, and General Motors car companies). If this were not the case, they were employed with one of the many suppliers who did business with the Big Three. Other manufacturing jobs were plentiful as well.

The unemployment rate was low. It seemed like a fairy tale to realize that a person did not have to have a high school diploma to get hired in the factories. These were mostly unskilled blue-collar positions that African-Americans held. Many that came from the south were unskilled in manufacturing and poorly educated. That did not matter as long as you could put a nut on a screw 50,000 times a day. Your knowledge of Shakespeare was wholly unnecessary.

Families were strong. In those days, families had mothers and fathers. If not, large extended families took up the slack of the traditional household. Everyone had a role to fill in the family unit. Neighbors even served as surrogate parents when necessary. People from the community often talked about what it was like growing up in the "good old days." They mention how a mischievous child could have been spanked for some misdeed by a neighbor. This time trial was followed up by the main race of which the Daytona 500 could not compare.

Social institutions like churches, community centers, and civic organizations flourished as well. The neighborhood was self-sufficient. It maintained itself. Black people had little options outside of the Black community for much.

Basic need concerns like food, shelter, and clothing were easily met. Perks of a middle-class lifestyle were common. As a matter of fact, many a college graduate owes a bit of gratitude to the money their parents made from the Big Three. They paid tuitions. This idyllic Detroit was soon to end. Foul race-relations would be the beginning of change in 1967.

Race-relations in Detroit were no love affair between Blacks and Whites. Lunch counters in many downtown department stores were still off limits for Blacks. Police patrolled the streets with very few African-American officers. There were neighborhoods that, as a Black person, you knew not to go to. An associate of mine recently purchased a home in one of the old affluent neighborhoods in Detroit. It is a few doors down from the Manogian Mansion- the home provided for the mayor of Detroit. The house's original deed read: "This house shall not come under the ownership of a Jew or a negro."

In the early morning of July 23, 1967, white police attempted a raid on an afterhours club: "Blind Pig." It seems that Black people were tired of that heavy-handed mistreatment. What ensued was 5 days of rioting that left 43 dead and 467 injured. Governor George Romney, the father of Mitt (former republican presidential candidate), called in the National Guard. Not to be out done, President Lyndon Johnson called in federal troops that drove tanks through city neighborhoods. Businesses were burned and looted. Many never rebuilt. That began the decline for Detroit.

" The core problem within the ghetto is the vicious circle created by the lack of decent housing, decent jobs, and decent education," wrote Kwame Ture and Charles V. Hamilton.

Whites left Detroit in droves. Areas that were exclusively White became exclusively Black. From its heyday in the 40's and 50's, Detroit lost 1/4 of its 1.5 million person population by the 90's. It went from the 4th largest city in the country to the 11th in a relatively short amount of time. Some neighborhoods were virtually abandoned. You could go blocks and see only one home amidst over grown vacant lots.

At nearly the same time, the manufacturing industry changed. Just as the assembly line created an employment increase, technological advances did the opposite. Williams Julius Wilson writes in his book, When Jobs Disappear, "In the 1970's nearly half of the huge unemployment declines for less-educated Blacks might be explained by the industrial shifts away from manufacturing towards other sectors." The jobs that had fed the children and purchased the cars, homes, and college tuitions were disappearing at a staggering rate.

What was happening in Detroit was happening across the North. In a twenty year period from 1967 to 1987, Philadelphia lost 64% of its manufacturing jobs; Chicago lost 60%; New York City, 58 %; Detroit, 51 %. In absolute numbers, these percentages represent the loss of 160,000 jobs in Philadelphia, 326,000 in Chicago, 520,000 in New York, and 108,000 in Detroit (Wilson, 1996, pg. 29-30.) A riot and massive job losses created the inner city ghetto in Detroit. The gas crisis of the early 70's added insult to injury.

High rates of joblessness trigger other neighborhood problems that undermined social organizations, ranging from crime, gang-violence, and drug trafficking to family breakups and problems in the organization of family life (Wilson, 1996, pg. 21). The illegal drug trade was arguably the worst consequence of the loss of work in Detroit. People looked to replace missing revenue. They wanted the financial security of this lucrative and highly dangerous enterprise.

Crack cocaine seeped into the inner city streets of Detroit in the 80's like poisonous gas from a car's tailpipe. In a city that had been deemed the murder capital of America in the 70's- drugs made it worse. Violent people in the crack-cocaine marketplace had a powerful influence on the social organization of a neighborhood….Drug Dealers cause the use and spread of guns in the neighborhood to escalate (Wilson, 2002, pg.21). Drug enterprises like Pony Down, 20/20, the Curry Brothers, the Best Friends, Young Boys Incorporated (ran by Butch Jones), White Boy Rick, and Maserati Rick were violent, treacherous, and deadly. Drug dealers in Detroit were ruthless and brazen; Maserati Rick was killed in his hospital room while recovering from an earlier shooting. Rohns Street was not sheltered from the gun violence. Growing up in the 70's in Detroit for some was like navigating a minefield wearing a blindfold.

I once awoke to the police investigating the murder of a young man found in between my house and another. Evidently, he had been left there like a broken-down old car. These types of things were a common occurrence. They happened all the time when I was growing up. Guns and gun violence was so common in Detroit that you could hear shots ring out at any time of the day or night. My family was not spared our neighborhood's favorite pastime. I was close to the junk yard many times myself.

Growing up, I loved the ageless Dick Clark. American Bandstand was one of my favorite programs. Watching young kids dance to the most popular songs in the country was a lot of fun. Seeing him officiate over the New Years Eve celebration in New York was a special treat. Checking out the youthful Clark and staying up late was pure excitement for a 10 year old.

Parked under our dining room table, one of my favorite hang outs, I watched the big shiny disco ball drop in Times Square. I was fascinated by the confetti, the celebrity guests, and all the couples lip-locked to celebrate the arrival of the New Year.

My weary eyes ushered me to bed. It was no longer than a few minutes when the sound of thunder rang through our house. Startled, I raced out the bed headed for the arms of my mother. My brother was headed in the same direction on his belly wobbling like a car with 4 flat tires.

We heard someone scurry off of our front porch in the commotion. Soon the police arrived to get the details. Our front living room window was shattered. There was a hole in the dining room wall the size of baseball. Lodged in the gas line of our stove was a quarter size piece of metal. It was a slug from a shotgun shell. We deduced that some lunatic had just fired a gun into our house. The path of that bullet still gives me shivers. It made a direct line from our front porch to the kitchen through the living and dining rooms. It cut right through where I was sitting under the table. My little body would have been mangled. It seemed that Rohns Street wanted to deposit another body not in between our house, but in it. This type of gun play occurred throughout the city, and my childhood.

Right on the corner of Rohns and Gratiot, at the end of the block, two guys had a disagreement. The matter was resolved with one man firing a bullet into the head of the other. He died right there on the spot. Later, a friend and I would search out the blood stain that was left on the sidewalk. As an adult, I found out that this was the perpetrator of the New Year's night shooting at my house. I guess this guy finally perfected his aim. He wasn't the only one.

Reggie, Johnny, and I decided to go to a party of a girl we grew up with when we were around 19 or 20 years old. The party was off of Rohns street. I was happy for the change in location. These girls had a thing for dating drug dealers. That was the first problem. As we sat in the party, we saw a guy walk in alone. He cruised around and greeted several people in the party. He was flamboyant and dressed well in a young Detroit drug dealer kind of way. He didn't notice the guys that promptly exited the party after they saw him. That was problem number two. After the guy had a bite to eat and said his final goodbyes he left. Shortly after, several gun shots rang out. We ran outside to see what had happened.

The guy who had just left the party was laying in the gutter. Dark red blood was flowing freely from several gunshot wounds like antifreeze from a cracked radiator. Several of us urged him on by saying, "come on man" and "hold on." We were young and dumb. What did we know? The ambulance never showed up and he died in the street like so many others. The housing complex where he was murdered was named after Martin Luther King Jr. The Dream had become a nightmare for many in Detroit. There were a number of times when the nightmare almost became mine.

One night my friend Reggie and I decided to go cruising by some clubs. We knew where we could find some nice looking ladies to eyeball. The Warehouse club was a 90's hotspot located on Woodbridge Street on the city's Eastside not far from the downtown area. The street was so narrow cars could barely drive past each other moving in opposite directions. As we navigated past the club that towered into the night sky on our right, we were virtually headlights to headlights with another car. One of us would have to back up so the other could pass. After a moment Reggie screamed, "Get the f$%^ out of the way." The car backed up and let us through. We thought that was the end of it.

We made a right turn and drove down to the traffic light at Jefferson and St. Aubin Street. I looked behind us and saw a car with its headlights turned off. That was a sure sign of trouble.

It was the car that had just allowed us to pass. They drove up next to us. There were 3 guys in the car. Two of them had guns. The driver reached his automatic pistol across the passenger and pointed at us. The guy in the back seat pumped the shotgun to automatically load a cartridge into the chamber. When we saw that, Reggie wasted no time and sped out into traffic through the red traffic light. Blam, blam, blam echoed like a car backfiring. By the time we made it to Reggie's house, his passenger side rear tire needed a mechanic. Better it than us. After that type of daring escape, one might imagine we would have stayed a long way from Woodbridge Street. It seems we liked flirting with the car compactor.

Reggie and I sat on the same street in a different car. My buddy had bought himself a brand new Honda Accord coupe. He was enjoying a boost in income from his job as a Detroit Fire Fighter. We drove by several clubs and ended up on the corner about to turn onto Woodbridge. Traffic was stop and go. It was packed. We had several cars behind us and a city block of cars in front of us. We weren't going anywhere fast.

A shabby dressed guy came up to Reggie's window. Feeling like Henry Ford himself in his new car, he politely rolled up his window in the guy's face. The guy came around to my window on the other side of the car. I can't remember what I said to the guy. Whatever it was, he didn't like it. He stepped back from the car and pulled up his shirt. The shiny 9mm pistol gleamed in the artificial light. My heart sunk. My throat tightened. My tough guy routine faded like a loud car radio as it moves further into the distance. I told Reggie to hurry and leave because the guy had a gun. We couldn't. We were trapped by the cars around us. My heart raced at the anticipation of it being made to stop. I thought I had come home from the corn fields on

Spring Break to die on the hard streets of the Motor City. The guy took another step back. That was it, I thought. My childhood and everyone I loved flashed before my eyes.

The guy looked fiendishly out of the corners of his eyes. At once, I recognized he was surveying who might see him. The deadly act was seemingly moments from happening. At that exact time thc car behind us moved. Instantly, Reggie put the car in reverse and floored it. We were flying down Dubois Street backwards like stuntmen in a Hollywood movie. We flew into Jefferson Ave like a rocket. The guy chased us all the way down the street. We ended up in the middle turn lane a few blocks away before our eruption of nervous laughter. We knew we had dodged a bullet, again, literally. The gun play never seemed to end.

Any idea of conflict resolution was foreign. Most of the time people didn't use it. It's hard to say if people had even heard of it. Maybe that was because many kids in the inner city were taught: if someone hits you, you hit them back. Mothers and Grandmothers were teaching this lesson. It was common place to see a child who had lost a fight to be marched back outside for round 2. That concept was outdated, foolish, and useless. It didn't work then and it doesn't work now. It could literally mean sending a kid out to a gun fight armed with nothing but his or her fists. Success was unlikely. There were other problems besides gun violence.

I had a friend around my age that had fathered 11 children, at last count. One child is a major time and money investment. Eleven is something akin to financing a professional basketball team. The idea of such a thing was unbelievable.

The idea of manhood had gotten bent in the chaos of the 70's and 80's. What it meant was a mystery to many young men and women. We had become a community that majored in minor things. Education was not one of the remedies for most.

I have seen people walking aimlessly back and forth down Rohns Street all day long. They will sit and talk on one end of the block. Then, they would mosey down to the other end like the walking dead. Even if someone had managed to scrape enough money to buy a car, they would ride around the neighborhood careful not to go too far. If not moving, they would sit in the car and listen to music and drink and smoke their cares away.

It was like the collective self-esteem and independence sought during the 60's was sucked out of Detroit during the 70's and 80's. "To establish true self-esteem we must concentrate on our successes and forget about failures and negatives in our lives," said public speaker and author Denis Waitley. If only this could be taught in schools, churches, and homes across Detroit city.

Besides financial mismanagement, the Detroit Public School system had been shrinking due to student departures. Year after year hundreds of students left for better educational opportunities. If that wasn't the case then parents left looking for better employment ones. In any event, schools were not getting the job done. Test scores represented that fact.

The dropout rate in DPS was around 50% at one time. That's a staggering rate of dysfunction. What could be more tragic than that? Rohns Street kids mirrored that average. As a matter of fact- I have seen people drop out of school in the 12th grade. The only obstacle was lack of desire.

My buddy would leave for school his senior year and not come back until around 3 o'clock. What he did during school time was heartbreaking. He would walk back and forth down Gratiot Avenue, the large street intersecting Rohns, for hours.

Whether rain, sleet, or snow, he was as committed as the postal service. Why he decided to do this, I have not the slightest idea.

Don't get me wrong. This is not the case for everyone in Detroit. As a matter of fact, some people would be hard pressed to understand what I'm talking about. At one time, Detroit had the largest Black middle-class in the country. Oakland County, which borders Detroit and Wayne County, was once one of the richest in the country. Some people in Detroit are still doing quite well.

Detroit, like most cites, has an alter ego. Million dollar homes still exist there. The problem is the gap in the distribution of wealth. The stark differences can be seen while driving down Mack Avenue on the city's Eastside. On one side, in the Indian Village neighborhood, you can pay over a million dollars for a mansion. On the other side of the street there are some homes that couldn't be given away.

Malcolm X said, "Education is the passport to the future, for tomorrow belongs to those who prepare for it today." If this is true, most of Detroit's kids are stuck in the present of never ending misery.

Detroit taught people to be violent. Handle your problems with your fists, a gun, but not your brain. I never bought into that mindset. Looking back at my childhood, I don't see why I didn't. I learned that I was not limited by the shortcomings of my neighborhood and city. What was necessary for my success was not where I was from, but where I was willing to go.

Chapter 8

BULLIES R US

I realized that bullying never had to do with you. It's the bully who's insecure. – Shay Mitchell

In the 70's and 80's owning a Schwinn bike made you a celebrity. They came in these vibrant and stunning colors combinations like green and yellow, red and yellow, and blue and gray. Rolls-Royce-like; the Schwinn name plate adorned the front of the bicycle frame. The Sting Ray model was unmistakable. They were the status symbol for kids who couldn't drive. My dream of owning one never came true.

You celebrity status vaulted towards the heavens if you could pop a wheelie and hold it. Some kids got so good at the maneuver; they would take off their front wheel. You would see them turning the corner of your block like a clown on a unicycle at the Barnum and Bailey Circus. My neighbor across the street was one of those daredevils.

The memory of my neighbor has not faded much. Some things become seared into your mind like a red-hot cattle brand. He was a chubby kid with a caramel complexion. His cornrows were knotted tight and drooped off of his head like the braches of a weeping willow. His teeth were jammed into his mouth like that of a great white shark. It was his words that tore at me and not his teeth.

When I would visit his sister, he would tear into me onsite. I suffered the most belittling, scathing, and venomous verbal tirades imaginable. Ugly, nappy-headed, black, and four-eyed were names hc repeated over and over. My 7 year-old eyes could rarely hold back the downpour of tears.

My mother would try and console me. She could not undo the damage that was being done to my self-esteem, confidence, and self-image. They were being smothered.

` When I look back on his behavior, I ask myself: "where were the adults?" "Where was my older brother?" I don't remember anyone stepping in on my behalf. It seems I was without protection. This is how life started for me on Rohns Street. I believe that self-esteem and self-confidence are like the transmission and engine of a car. If they get damaged, you are in for serious trouble.

I can remember being threatened by one of the Washington kids on Holcomb Street on the next block behind us. I was so terrified, I would take the long way down Gratiot Avenue and nearly double the distance to Stephens elementary just to avoid this kid. The fear was real. The impact to my inner self was too. It would take decades for me to repair the damage that had been done.

Chapter 9
THE WONDER YEARS

I think writing is such a great talent, and if I was better, I would love to be a writer. – Shiloh Fernandez

"Royce," My teacher said proudly.

Passing out test scores for her must have been part torture and part ecstasy. She was giddy in a "my students are doing well" kind of way after calling my name. I wasn't the only one. Many of my classmates gave her that same fuzzy feeling inside.

I streaked up to her desk and received my CAT scores. CAT stood for California Achievement Test. There were standardized tests even in the 70's. Why we took a test from California I never would know. It's probably the same reason later I would take the ACT for college made in Iowa City, IA. I guess Detroit public school administration believed this one was best for us at the time. The high-stakes, 'everything rests on this' kind-of tests wouldn't come along for another decade.

At the time, I didn't see the big deal. I had scored in the high 90th percentile in math and reading. This was the 2rd year I did so. I wasn't the only one either. Usually, it was about 4 or 5 of us who scored prodigy-high. That wasn't the only time I shocked the towering adult masses at Stephens Elementary school on Detroit's Eastside.

One day I was mysteriously taken out of class.

"Leave all your things", I was told.

I didn't see my momma's smiling face so I knew something wasn't right. I was baffled because I didn't remember pulling an unusual number of ponytails or pissing too much on the bathroom floors that day. We weren't on course to the 6-fingered assistant principal's office, Mr. Eddy, either. He had an extra little baby finger sticking out of each hand. He was medium build about 5'10" and in his late 30's or early 40's. He wore the standard 70's gear. His tight little afro was well maintained. His beard was a little scruffy though. Imagine Eddie Monster meets Eddie Murphy meets George Jefferson. He was good to us nevertheless.

The giants ushered me into an empty library. Five or six brown round tables waited for me. Tiny red, blue, and green chairs sat surrounding the table all neat and organized. Wooden book shelves lined the walls. Black wire columns of See Jane Run-type books sat nicely in there. Ms. Jeter ran her library like a drill sergeant. This portly caramel-covered lady could wield a paddle too. You forgot the Dewey decimal system at your own peril. These were the corporal punishment days, the good old days. She wasn't there. At least, I didn't see her.

"Have a seat Royce", I was politely asked.

"Here is a piece of paper and a pencil," the lady said. "I can see that" I thought.

"You wrote a very nice poem in English class." She said apprehensively.

I had written a simple- I thought- little poem about a butterfly in class. I had forgotten about it. Is this really why I'm here, I wondered.

"We want you to write another poem," she continued.

What the "heck", I thought. "Heck" was one on my 5 cent words I generally used. The 25 cent variety, I used on the playground and to entertain my brother's friends. Sailors could not curse like I could. My intellect made me proficient in weaving long streams of profanity and poetry, as it seemed.

It took me all of 10 minutes to write an eight line poem about a bear. Frost it wasn't. Astounding for a little black nappy-headed kid from Rohns Street, it was. They went on to publish these two poems in a district-wide publication of outstanding student work. Years later, I would look back at these events with strong feelings.

My high standardized test scores and writing skills didn't lead me to the talented and gifted school. I wasn't placed in the honors class with other little prodigies at Stephens Elementary. There was no after school program for me. Teachers didn't even give me more challenging work. The only practice I remember for smart kids was double promotion. Nothing special happened for me to cultivate my talent. My abilities were left alone in that shiny and neat little library on the Eastside of Detroit, at the corner of Burns and Lambert.

I wandered through school. Sometimes, I was a great student. At other times, it seemed like I didn't know what end of the pencil to use. I was like a boat cast adrift. There was no direction, no focus, and no purpose. I didn't have an oar in the water. Looking back, I wonder what could have been if provision had been made for me and my talent.

Could a talented and gifted school have taught me the other things: organization, time management, or focus? Maybe, I could have learned somewhere along the way to pick my friends better. Possibly, someone could have defined "drive" for me. Lastly, most importantly, perhaps I could have built healthy self-esteem and self-confidence. When and where I lived made that a very difficult proposition. Self-esteem was hard to come by in the heart of the inner city. It was even harder to find in middle school.

Barbour middle school was about a 10 block walk from my house. We were lucky to be able to take the bus. It was the feeder school for about 4 elementary buildings. It was big. It was wild. After getting into several fights and threatened by several bullies, my mom moved me to another school. Whatever her issues, she saw that I needed a change. It probably saved my academic life.

When I entered Whitney Young, I befriend kids like me. These were kids whose parents wanted something better for them. I flourished. My behavior and grades soared. Those two years of success led me to the city's flagship high school. Green and white never looked so good.

Chapter 10
THOSE CASS TECHNICIANS

Self-esteem is the reputation we acquire with ourselves – Nathaniel Branden

"Green, green, green, green, green and white," echoed throughout the ancient gym. It was built in a time when they were called gymnasiums. Nine floors was large for a high school, but not for Cass Technical High school. Unfounded rumors said that our building had once been a pickle factory. Lending itself to the reason why the school colors were green and white. It was a mountainous building that stretched over an entire city block in both directions. Scores of windows peered out over Detroit in every direction. It was bigger than some of the buildings in downtown.

It was named after William Cass who served as governor of the Michigan territory from 1813 to 1831. He donated the land where cows used to graze on the outskirts of town. The building that I haunted was opened in 1922. My mother and grandmother had both been students there as well. They weren't the only notables to grace those hallways.

Diana Ross, Lily Tomlin, John DeLorean, and jazz greats Earl Kluge and Donald Byrd had all been Technicians. Charles Lindberg's mother taught chemistry there for over 10 years. Many other mayors, police chiefs, and Detroit political figures had studied there too. The student body was diverse in the early 80's.

Students from all over the metropolitan Detroit area went to Cass. Students of different racial, ethnic, and religious backgrounds made for a very eclectic and cosmopolitan campus. We were known for being smart, preppy, and good-looking. That was true at least until I arrived in 1983.

My behavior at Cass Tech was wild on a good day. On a bad day it was downright dangerous. When there is a problem on the inside there will always be a problem on the outside. I can remember popping fire crackers in one of my classroom's waste baskets when the teacher stepped out. No one dared to tell. The foolish "no snitching" policy was in effect even then. I can remember shooting skyrockets down the hallway. How no one ever got hurt is beyond me. Not even teachers were safe from my senseless behavior.

As a freshman, I got a chance to assist my homeroom teacher, Mrs. Blake, with yearbook coordination. She was the sponsoring faculty member and would have us in the class during lunchtime and study hour. Ms. Blake was one part Pam Grier, one part Vanessa Williams, and all part beautiful. One day I had the nerve to mention the tight fit of her Jordache jeans on her butt. She threatened to slap the black off of me.

Because Cass was the flagship high school of the district, we would be visited by numbers of professional athletes, politicians, and celebrities. On this particular occasion one such celebrity came to tape a concert of his new songs for a national cable company. The problem was that the auditorium was not large enough for the entire student body. Someone decided that my class was not going. I decided that I was.

When school was dismissed early, a band of rejects hovered around in the bathroom. When the hallways were clear, we made our way to the auditorium making sure to hug the walls like we were dodging enemy fire. At the site of an administrator, adult, or hall monitor, we would sprint up or down the stairway and into a bathroom or back hallway. The building was cavernous and made our detection and capture highly unlikely.

When we made it to the hallway near the auditorium, we tried to pry the door open. To our surprise, we found some escapees already hiding in the shadows. We were in the back of the balcony. Twenty kids enjoying the perks of Cass "Techness." The music sounded great. The performer was a decent singer and musician. He had a couple of hits here and there. I wonder if Stevie Wonder knew he had fans in the balcony. "I just called to say I love you….."

Cass Tech had a great sports tradition. I knew that. I wanted to be a part of it. Black boys from the hood only want to play one or two sports: basketball and football. I didn't really care for basketball even though I could run and jump with the best of them. I hadn't played that much and had little skills. Football was a different story.

I had more talent than confidence. Unfortunately one without out the other isn't a recipe for success in anything, especially sports. That was my high school football career in a nutshell. I did get pretty strong and fast for a high school freshman. However, I was missing the vital ingredient. I'm sure that having high self-confidence and self-esteem at that vital time would have sent my athletic career in a different direction. The success of every endeavor a person undertakes hinges on how they see themselves. I never played a game at Cass Tech or was even given a uniform.

Sneaking through hallways, staging fireworks displays, and being a blithering idiot caught up to me. There was a grade point average requirement to remain at Detroit's flagship high school. I didn't achieve it. I was academically dismissed. I had flunked out of Cass Tech. Tears filled my eyes as my counselor told me the verdict. I had done it to myself. This was a self-inflicted wound. Time after time I would play Russian Roulette with my future, and lose.

My focus wasn't on grades- it was on perception. I cared more about how my friends saw me than my grades. I wanted to stick out at school because my home life was spinning out of my control. I should have found the right friends to impress. Those who aspired to attend the University of Michigan, Harvard, or Yale should have been the crowd I sought.

The schoolwork was not too hard for me to do. I was definitely smart enough. My failure at Cass Tech had nothing to do with academics. It had everything to do with effort. My mother's illness had impacted my self-esteem like a ten car pileup. It mangled me on the inside. I heard a person once say: "you will never achieve higher than your self-esteem." I was proof of that.

Chapter 11

WELCOME TO THE JUNGLE, KETTERING HIGH SCHOOL

Instilling a sense of self-discipline and focus when the kids are younger makes it so much easier by the time they get to high school – Amy Chua

The eight block walk to Kettering high school happened without much fanfare. It was made more enjoyable when chatting with one of my buddies. After making the left at the end of Rohns Street, you could see the huge blue cement "K" in front of the school in the distance down Lambert Street. On this particular morning of my senior year, things were different.

As you approached the school, students normally would be milling around socializing. That was not the case this morning. On Lambert, unmarked police cars lined both sides of the street for an entire block preceding the building on Van Dyke Avenue. We had learned to spot unmarked police cars like a bloodhound. It was a skill we learned growing up in the Hood.

There is about 60 meters from Van Dyke to the school's front doors. In that area are cement blocks that served as seats.

Half of a football field could have fit in that area. No students were waiting there either. Seeing several uniformed Detroit police officers frighten me. It was eerily quiet for a high school of over 1,500 students.

As students walked up to the school, officers made sure they did not turn around. They barked out directions like drill sergeants. We were wrangled into the school. Students were noticeably shaken. This was true for the guilty and the not so guilty. Kettering was one of the roughest schools in the district. This wasn't Cass Tech. Kids brought more to school than argyle socks and penny loafers.

We were corralled around a circular hallway with no working windows or doors. Our library was in the middle. No police were monitoring this area since there was no way out. At the end of this hallway a metal detector was set up. Officers checking our bags like we had been caught shoplifting. Kids were on the verge of tears. I was too. It was scarier than the shootouts that occasionally happed at the school.

There were more police than I had ever seen in my life. It took a while to figure out what was going on. We were being treated like hardened criminals. It was one of the most traumatic events of my childhood. You couldn't tell if we were in a school or a warzone. Unfortunately, both were the case.

This was the first weapons and contraband sweep I experienced at Charles F. Kettering high school. This huge production caught a few kids with marijuana. A bounty of contraband and weapons were found behind radiators on the floor around the unmonitored library. Quick-thinking students ditched there illegal items behind a long radiator that surrounded the library where we were being herded. There were enough guns found that day to start your very own arsenal. This was not a safe learning environment to say the least.

Mr. Jones was the principal. He smelled like a liquor store every day. If he wasn't an alcoholic, he wore the worst cologne of all time. I'm surprised he kept his job for over 20 years. We don't know how he was able to function. He slurred his words, stumbled every once in a while, and was absent during most important school events. We would take his lead and run with it.

"Blue, blue, blue, blue, blue, and white," we yelled in drunken glee. Over 200 ounces of malt liquor had been consumed by the time we made it to the boy's varsity basketball game. Mr. Wiggen's party store was just a block from the front doors of the school. Buying booze was easy. We just got someone from the neighborhood hanging around the store to buy it for us. Back then I didn't care what I put into my body. I didn't yet recognize that alcohol abuse was a symptom of my low self-esteem. Most drunks want to escape their reality because they don't like it.

Reggie, Mario, Guch, and I were doing the wave with only 4 people. We were sitting apart from the crowd. We looked crazy. Who cared? We were having a ball, we thought. Basketball games at Kettering high school were athletic social events. We were feeling real social. It was the first time I had gotten drunk at school. I was in the 11th grade. We enjoyed other "good" times as well.

Ms. Tibbs was my physics teacher during my senior year. She was one of the prettiest teachers at school. I adored her. She was petite, always dressed nice, and had her hair flowing like Rapunzel. One day in class, she was writing something on the board. Unexpectedly, she turned around, looked at me, and said, "Royce you are so cute." I was amazed. We were astonished. To hear something like that from a teacher was unbelievable. When I run into people from that class, 30 years later, they commonly mention this incident. If I believed her that could have really been a big self-confidence booster. But, I didn't. It was hard to believe anything good about myself.

Each year, a sleigh ride and hay ride were sponsored by the senior class. As juniors, we were thrilled at the prospect of joining the festivities- being taken to a rustic farm over an hour outside of Detroit made it much more fun. We had the entire place to ourselves. Marshmallows roasting, bond fires, and rides on a horse-drawn wagon were scheduled activities. The real fun was of course digesting alcohol, chasing girls, and acting like crazed maniacs. Of which, I showed great skill. I had to show I was good at something, even though it was bad.

The bus ride to the farm consisted entirely of drinking. I walked across Gratiot to the grocery store and purchased my liquor. They didn't even ask me for identification. Don Q was a Puerto Rican rum. At 120 proof- it could start your car, remove paint, and straighten curly hair. We drank half the bottle by the time we made it to the farm. I quite literally stumbled off of the bus.

During one of the hayrides, we decided to spice up the marshmallow roasting time. As people stood around the fire, we would take piping hot marshmallows off of the sticks and smash them in their faces and hair. Drunken shrieks rose up and pierced the night sky like a wolf howling at the moon. That lasted for what seemed like hours. I wasn't immune to the devilment. While laughing at someone else's misfortune; one of my friends reached around my face and smashed a handful of molten hot, gooey, marshmallows in my face. It took months to get all of that stuff out of my glasses.

We brought along water guns as well. Who didn't like to play with water guns? To add our own distinctive flair; we decided to fill them with refined malt liquor processed by our own human machinery... we pissed in the water guns. No one knew what we were doing besides 4 or 5 of my closest friends. People ducked and dodged the streams with little success. We named it a KE golden shower (short for Kettering). Even chaperones weren't immune from our drunken tomfoolery.

There was a nice-sized log cabin that served as the mess hall. There were around 7 or 8 nice-sized picnic-styled tables inside. You could easily seat 50 people in there at a time. They had prepared hot dogs, hamburgers, and the usual camping/picnic foods. While we were preparing to eat, one of my friends did something that baffles me even today.

Liquored up and flowing with adolescent hormones, he grabbed the crotch of one of the chaperones. We were shocked. She slapped him hard enough to rearrange his dental work. Even though he was sharply verbally chastised; he was not suspended or expelled from school. Today, he would have been on vacation for the rest of the school year and maybe even charged with sexual assault. What made it worse was that the victim was one of our classmates' mother.

Underage drinking was a huge problem for us. We didn't understand the connection between drinking and making bad choices. It is no coincidence that many crimes are committed while intoxicated. I can't count the number of times I was in a car when the driver had been drinking. Lives had been cut short and families forever destroyed because of what we did so carelessly. We enjoyed skipping school as much as we did going.

Virtually every Monday during the spring semester of our senior year, we skipped school. Several of us had physics with

Ms. Tibbs first hour. We didn't want to miss that. After the first hour we would slip out the back door and pile into one of our friends' car. Robert Baitler allowed 5 to 6 unruly kids in his car at once. Usually, we drove to the West side of Detroit so as not to be detected by any of our family members. Fairlane Mall was usually where our limousine service dropped us off. At the time, they didn't care about children hanging around the mall during school hours. Movies were the best way to pass the time.

The science-fiction movie *Aliens* had just been released. There is a part in the movie where a little girl, Knut, is speaking about the alien monsters and says: "They mostly come out at night, mostly." It sounded like she was saying "moshly." We found that gut-bustingly, knee-slappingly hilarious. "Moshly" became our tagline for the rest of the year. Twenty plus years later, you may hear one of use repeating that line. A good deal of the time we would head back to school after the movies.

All of us were on the track team except my friend David Carter. Mike, Robert, Reggie, and I would always come back to school and go to track practice. On one particular day we had been drinking. I was a hurdler in high school. It's a very technical event. Running over ten 39 inch barriers with only 3 steps between is pretty difficult. Alcohol consumption does not make it easier. It makes it downright dangerous. I knocked over several hurdles and sprained my ankle. Coach Gill didn't know what was going on. I didn't either. In high school we didn't see drinking for what it was.

I started binge drinking when I was in the 10th grade. It started in a friend's basement and continued until I was well into my 30s. We were able to get our hands on alcohol very easily. It was never difficult; our parents had it around, someone would buy it for us, or we would buy it for ourselves. To say we abused alcohol is an understatement. I wonder how many of my high school classmates would become addicted, suffer medical problems, or die from alcohol abuse. Thankfully, my alcohol abuse didn't stop me from graduating high school. I flourished at Kettering despite the problems.

Academically, my time at Kettering was in contrast with my time at Cass Tech. My friends were important, but my grades were more important. By happenstance, I started several great habits. First was my fortress of solitude. Our kitchen was a great place to study. After all the cooking was done, I would close the door and have several hours with no interruptions. A straight back chair and a table that Gramps kept spotless were all I needed. It was well lit, enough space, and quiet. I sat there until all of my school work was done. If I had time afterwards, I would go outside and hang out with my friends.

My school friends were mischievous like I was; but we were not delinquents. Birds of a feather flock together… so the saying goes. We didn't know it then, but we were one of the main reasons that each other had graduated high school at all. None of us became part of the insane dropout rate. There were school friends and neighborhood friends. Some of my neighborhood friends were tragically different.

Tito and I met at Stephen's elementary school. He lived two blocks away. You could see the school from his backyard. From what I remember- his mom had died when he was real young. His father was a Joseph Stalin kind of strict. Tito would tell me how his dad would give him serious spankings when he got into trouble at school. What you put in a kid at some point will always come out.

In high school, he fell in with the wrong crowd. These were dope boys. Dope boys sold drugs and made more money than your parents did at the car companies. They had the nicest cars, prettiest girls, and the worst dispositions. Getting on their bad side could be fatal. Detroit's title as murder capital of the country was evidence of that. Tito was still my friend anyway. We played with toys together in his backyard when life was so very simple. During my senior year, he came to me with a proposition.

Tito introduced me to one of those dope boys. He seemed like a nice guy. He drove a plain jeep without shiny wheels or loud music. This "plain guy" said that he would give us some drugs to sell up front and that we could pay him back with the money we made. We were assured that there would be plenty left over to keep. It had been less than two months since our lights and water had been turned back on. I had no money. This seemed foolproof. Nothing ever is, though.

What would make an honor student agree to sell drugs? I lived in an environment of intense poverty. In the late 80's and 90's the car companies were rocking and reeling from a recession. Drug and alcohol addiction along with unemployment could be found in most of the houses on Rohns street. There were times when people on my street didn't even have enough to eat. Those were the years of not enough. Those were the times of desperation. Desperate people will do anything to relieve their pain.

Tito and I were to wait for our first drop-off of drugs. We talked about what we would do with all the money. Fantasizing about a better life with pretty girls on our arms and new clothes on our backs, we waited. Days turned in to weeks. Tito came to meet me with some important news. Fortunately (in hindsight) our would-be drug boy boss was pulled over by the police on a routine traffic stop. He, his plain jeep, and our drugs were all confiscated. That was the last we ever heard of our own private Pablo Escobar. I shudder to think of what may have happened to my life had I started peddling drugs in the most dangerous city in America as a 17 year old. Tito would inevitably continue down his own dark path without me.

Detroit had many gangs of dope boys. Tito kept looking until he found a home. Those relationships would land him in and out of jail for several years. Even dope boys get their 15 minutes of fame, though. On an episode of a nationally broadcast TV show: "America's Dumbest Criminals" Tito was shown robbing a bank after just leaving it. He didn't even bother to change his clothes. Needless to say, he was arrested. I never looked to selling drugs again and kept my eyes fixed firmly on school.

My strong relationships with my track and football coaches as well as my teachers were vital to my success at KE. They were great. I loved coming to school- even though I skipped from time to time. I often went to teachers when I needed help. They liked that. I needed help with physics often.

My grades soared. I carried over a 3.5 grade point average my last year in high school. I managed my time wisely. I never knew that time management was a key to long-lasting success. That information would help me later on in my life. "You don't have time to do everything," author and public speaker, Brian Tracy once said. "But, you do have time to do the most important things first," He concluded. That's what I did, and that made a real difference.

Ms. Howard in the counseling office was very helpful. On one of my several trips to see her in my senior year- a black and gold information booklet caught my attention. I was a huge Pittsburgh Steelers fan as a kid and I subsequently loved those colors. It had two applications in it: one for admission and one for housing. They both had "SSS" on the top. That made them free to submit. Months later, I would learn what those three S's meant. I was special and definitely in need of support services. My counselor greased the wheels for my entrance into college.

Mr. Tomlin was cool as a fan. He was a member of a black fraternity called Kappa Alpha Psi. They were known for their good looks and laid back personalities. On a visit to see him after I had graduated from high school, he told me some interesting information. When my university requested my school file, he made it seem more "appealing." I'm glad he did. There would be other guardian angels along my route to success. We all have them. My keys to success in high school were suddenly so clear.

I didn't realize it at the time; but there was a plethora of people who were vital to my success. Parents and relatives, school friends, teachers, administrators, and coaches all helped me along the way. They all brought something meaningful, positive, and necessary to my life. They were givers, not takers. No relationship can last long if people just take and do not give. There has to be some reciprocity. When I had learned better later on in life, I stayed away from these people like The Plague. In any event, I succeeded from my good mentors. They were essential.

I had improved academically because I had become a good student. It's not that I had become any smarter per se; but I learned strategies and behaviors that made my success possible. Getting good grades had more to do with these strategies and behaviors than intellect. A quiet well-lit place was key. Asking for help when I needed it was just as important. The stage was set.

GRADUATE

In June of 1987, I was in a great position. Graduation day from high school was right around the corner. Mostly by luck, I had avoided every pitfall commonly found in the ghetto. There were no pregnancies, criminal records, substance abuse, financial troubles, truancy issues, or academic failures severe enough to keep me away from my cap and gown. I had sidestepped them all. Even my binge drinking couldn't stop me. I did however have another issue that could have changed the direction of my life forever.

The last part of the brain to develop is the frontal lobe- also known as the reasoning center. We are usually able to vote, obtain a driver's license, legally drink alcohol, and fight in our country's wars before it is fully developed. It is why young people commonly make some serious mistakes in judgment. Many of these mistakes can never be undone. We are then forced to deal with their consequences for the rest of our lives.

On Rohns Street and in the ghettos and barrios across our country; three traits are highly respected for young men: athleticism, violence, and hypersexuality. Being smart was low on the totem pole. On many occasions it was the cause for ridicule, bullying, and isolation. Growing up in the Hood- young men better be good at one of the three or they would have a rocky childhood. Sometimes, I think I was raised in an anti-universe.

In this universe, things that were good were seen as bad and vice-versa. Boys shunned concord for conflict, books for basketballs, and self-restraint for self-indulgence. I believe this is due to low community self-esteem and self-worth. It was like an airborne disease. Many families tried hard to guide their boys in the right direction. As soon as they left the protective bubble of their homes, they were infected. So was my prognosis.

It was commencement day. Graduates were to meet at KE in the evening for the ceremony. I started the day off foolishly by trying to raise my low self-esteem. We slid girls in the backdoor of my friend Brian's house- undetected by his parents. Becky and I were seniors at Kettering. We were both Cass Tech rejects. Brian was a junior at Murray Wright High School who didn't mind skipping. When his mom was at work, we would "explore" girls down in his basement, undisturbed. She was known by some older guys in our neighborhood. They told us about her exploits. I never knew she was so talented when she was my girlfriend earlier that school year. That wasn't my only sexual escapade during my senior year.

My experience with Teri a few months earlier did little to slow down or stop my wanton sexual behavior. By the time I graduated, I had had sexual experiences with at least 5 girls. That was normal for boys during that time. Sexually transmitted diseases and potential pregnancies were not a part of my thought process at that point. Chasing and catching girls was the way that my injured self-esteem sought for my elusive manhood. It would take me many years to recognize that I could not "find myself" in a woman's bed.

Chapter 12

TERI THE FIRST "LOVE"

When you're a teenager, you want to meet a lot of girls; you want to get the most girls. You don't know anything about respect; you don't know anything about being faithful and loyal to your girlfriend. – Nas

I believe that via some awful coding error in my DNA- I may have picked up my daddy's womanizing ways. Maybe my hood education taught me how to behave with the opposite sex. I'm sure it was a combination of the two. When I met Teri I was to learn such important life lessons. We were introduced through a childhood friend- Tracey. Tracey and I had gone to elementary and middle school together. Her house was two blocks away from mine and down the street from Tito. Tracey and I had both flunked out of Cass Tech. Despite this, we still maintained our friendships with our former classmates. Teri was one of those friends.

Teri and I were both seniors when we met. I had just quit the football team and suddenly had time on my hands. All three of us went out to the movies and there was an immediate attraction between us. Teri was pretty. I liked that. She had a nice shape.

I liked that too. She was skilled in the fine arts of boys as well. I really liked that.

During the fall of our senior year, we would rendezvous over at her house. Half-days provided us with the opportunity to mess around. Her mother was at work and my parents didn't keep track of my school schedule. The concept of safe sex did not exist yet for me. Sadly, condom use did not happen for me until I was well into college. It would eventually be my cousin- and not my parents- who would teach me about prophylactics.

My older cousin Gary had showed me what a condom was back in our old garage. He all but put on the old looking balloon that he kept in his wallet. It left a ring imprint in the leather. I don't think he knew that you weren't supposed to take it out of the wrapper until use. I did have some sex education training, though.

Joyce Elaine gave me the birds and bees talk when I was around five years old. She pulled out an encyclopedia and showed me what all of the working parts looked like. They looked like buck-naked cartoons to me. I couldn't grasp what all of that meant. Yet, I commend my mother for doing the best she could to raise her two sons responsibly. For that, I will always love her and am eternally grateful.

There were sex education classes at Charles F. Kettering High School. That was the only class we didn't skip. They were gender specific- composed of all boys or all girls. We didn't play the bathroom pass revolving door game either. Students didn't insistently ask for a bathroom pass to kill time in those lessons. Many of the boys never left their seats, as a matter of fact. I don't think the girls' teacher was as good as ours- our class president was pregnant by Christmas.

It seems that our teacher wasn't that good either because Teri was pregnant by Thanksgiving. I wasn't afraid probably because I didn't grasp the seriousness of the situation. When I told my parents, I expected a cry of outrage to rise up like smoke from a burning building. There was none. I was shocked.

My grandmother gave birth to my mom at the ripe old age of 15. At least Teri was 17. When Teri came to meet my parents, she was petrified. She didn't even speak. I thought that was strange until I recounted the situation in my mind recently. I could not imagine being 17, pregnant, and "solely" responsible for another life. What a heavy burden to carry.

Her mother made the appointment and paid for the abortion. I was too afraid to go with Teri because I didn't want to face her mother. I cannot actually recall if I met her mother or not. Our ages showed. I could not imagine being 17, an expecting father, and "partly" responsible for another person. The idea is overwhelming now, and was impossible to comprehend then.

Then, teen-aged pregnancy was one of the major reasons for girls to drop out of high school. Today, more girls are staying in school and completing their high school diploma. Efforts were made to combat the problem of teenage pregnancy. There are now schools that cater to girls who are pregnant or have children. These schools are a necessity and a very noble effort.

I used sex to address my low self-esteem. I'm not the first to do so, or the last. The phenomenon is not relegated to just men. Many women suffer from this problem as well. Documentary filmmaker Ray Upchurch called the behavior "Daddy Hunger". This hunger is caused by girls being raised in homes where the love from a custodial male is not psychologically sufficient. Conversely, I would suppose a "mommy hunger" of sorts exists in parallel. Whatever the case; it's important for parents to actively grow, cultivate, and protect the self-esteem of their children. Otherwise, problems will occur. Is this issue more nature or nurture?

I wonder how much of my father's womanizing DNA was coded within my body. He had five children by 3 different women (that we know of). Does it make a difference? Is this an excuse to justify my reckless behavior? I'm not sure. What I do know is that I had participated in risky behavior regardless.

Teenage pregnancy was so rampant in my neighborhood; it was a mere trifle to find out that someone was pregnant. It was as shocking as having wheat toast instead of white. More than half the girls in my neighborhood had a baby or got pregnant during high school. Virtually all of them that had babies dropped out of school. In those days there were no special programs to combat the problem of teenage pregnancy. There was only Similac, creamed peas, and days spent at home wondering where one's youth had gone.

In the early eighties HIV/AIDS had just found a name. I neither cared, was aware, or curbed my behavior. HIV/AIDS and other STDs were simply not a factor in my thinking. Reckless abandon represented my behavior too, mildly. We just didn't care. The urge to embody our idea of manhood was stronger than anything I learned in class. Fathering children for young men was like a badge of honor for some. Taking care of them was another story.

One of my friends couldn't count the number of children he had fathered on two hands. It seems unbelievable, but he is almost running out of toes too. Men in the hood were having kids all over the place. A good number of men 18 or older were someone's "Baby Daddy." Being a father was another matter. Neither of which I would become. How I avoided STDs, parenthood, dropping out of high school, jail, or death can only be attributed to how well Ruth Alberta Kinniebrew could pray. Grace and mercy led me to the defining period of my life.

Chapter 13

BURGE RESIDENCE HALL

In college you either find yourself or lose yourself – Royce Kinniebrew

The mascot for the University of Iowa- Herky the Hawk- attended pep rallies, parades, and sporting events. Miraculously, he swooped around campus being in more than one place at a time. He could be at a football game whilst simultaneously visiting children at the Iowa Hospitals and Clinics. School mascots were sweet and mysterious like that.

Several people sported the Black and Gold costume in my day. As a matter of fact, it may have required four separate people during the course of a football game to maintain high energy while wearing the costume. Delta Tau Delta fraternity members had been the bodies behind the mask. Their house was directly across Johnson Street from Burge Hall. Their school spirit must have rubbed off on me.

While I never wore the costume with the winged arms and hawk head; I did own plenty of university paraphernalia. Walking into Burge Hall, one of my new friends, Paris Lewis, made the remark: "Here comes the Black Herky the Hawk!" That was enough to get laughs from everyone sitting down in the lobby. I was only wearing Iowa sweat pants, a sweat shirt, hat, and socks. Then, they didn't sell Hawkeye shoes. I was suffering from an identity crisis. Who I was at the time was rather unclear to me. I needed to become Herky because I did not really know Royce. So I bought enough Iowa gear to reinvent myself.

My friends, nor I, knew that secretly I didn't like myself. As a matter of fact, I may have hated myself. I tried to makeover the outside because I wasn't fond of what was on the inside. People spend thousands of dollars to do so. It never works. Sooner or later, what's on the inside will uncover itself. All my words and deeds came from a place of fear and self-hate. It would take me 10 years of undergraduate education, self-discovery, improving my skills as a student, and repairing my low self-esteem to become a college graduate. That decade would set the course for the rest of my life. Until then, I had to feed the beast. I had to be the wildest, drunkest, most lascivious person I could imagine. Burge Hall was a good place to start.

Walking down the hallway coming back from dinner, I noticed several guys streaming back and forth into one of the dorm rooms. As I got close to the action, one of my hall mates ushered me in the room with a devilish smile. "Hey Sugar, check this out" he said. I entered a dark room with 20 plus guys crowded around the window like kids outside of a toy store. The "oohs" and "aahs" leapt up from the voyeurs like cheers at a fireworks celebration.

Burge Residence Hall on the Campus of the University of Iowa was built in one of those weird Cold War paranoid 50's styles. The building had 5 floors and 4 wings in my day. We were the 4th wing on the 5th floor, the 4500s. A bird's eye view would have shown that it looked like the letter "E" with an extra parallel bar. Each wing was gender specific. The wings were exposed as well. A person on the 4th wing could see clearly into the rooms on the 3rd wing. At night it was like looking at a wall full of HD TVs. That night we watched a pay-per-view movie, if you will.

One floor down, on the female wing, some poor girl left her shades open and her lights on. That was a bad move. I don't know what was worse: Eavesdropping on someone having sex, or eavesdropping on someone having sex while drinking and snorting drugs. This couldn't have gotten any better for college guys. It did. We savored the folly for several minutes before I got a dim idea. "Let's go down there," I said.

It was easy to figure out what room this girl and guy were in because the wings were virtually identical. I led the march down to her room like Sherman on his scorched earth campaign. Leading 20 or 30 guys through the narrow hallways was intoxicating. The climax was what occurred when we got there. I had to make this moment memorable.

I knocked on the door for several minutes. They probably needed time to hide the drugs and alcohol. Opening the door, her eyes bulged with the surprise of seeing a hallway full of guys. I performed brilliantly for the occasion. Dramatically, I shouted, "The next time you decide to get high and have sex you should close your blinds!" Quickly she sobered up, turned to the window, looked back at me in terror, and slammed the door in my face. The guys chanted "Sugar, Sugar, Sugar!" all the way back to our floor. Drug and alcohol abuse would cause embarrassment and heartache for many people in Burge Hall.

Jersey was a guy who hailed from the Garden State. He was the John Belushi, Chris Farley, and Jonah Hill of our floor. He was fat, merry like Santa Claus, and drank like a thirsty fish.

He would drink in the middle of the day during the week. To call him an alcoholic may be an understatement.

One evening around 7 or 8, he was passed out on his bed. By the time I had gotten to him, others had already written things in marker on his face. This would commonly happen to those who passed out when most others were sober. People would write things like: loser, drunk, mama's baby, whore, and fool on their body, often the face. People would even write in permanent marker, which it really wasn't. It was just really hard to get off. The funniest inscriptions were written backwards on the person's forehead- similar to how "Ambulance" is written on the front of those vehicles so motorists can read it in their rearview mirrors. Likewise, when the drunkard would awaken and look in the mirror- he or she would have an immediately legible note from their attackers. We had a prank to play on Jersey.

I was to aggravate him until he chased me into the hallway. One of my hall mates would be waiting. I think I licked my finger and shoved it into his ear. "Quit it Sugar!" he howled. I kept up the pestering until he staggered to his feet and gave chase. I ran out the room and ran down the hallway. When he exited his room to follow, he got splashed with a garbage can full of water from the other direction. He laughed a drunken laugh and staggered back to his bed soaking wet. In but a few moments he was back to sleep. Let's try it again I thought. He fell for the prank at least 2 more times before we stopped. It just wasn't funny anymore. It was sad. Mass drunkenness was as common as solo, lonely drunkenness.

Gargantuan, Colossal, and Gigantic, were all names of parties we threw in Burge Hall on our wing. These parties were not particularly small- as their names might suggest. They were large in duration, imagination, population, and consumption. I came up with the idea of naming these parties. We wanted them to be remembered. They were to go down in history as grand events of drunken tomfoolery. They did just that. We needed only one magic ingredient to make it happen: booze.

John's Grocery was the spot where most of the campus went to buy alcohol. Nicknamed Dirty Johns- for what reason I do not know- it sold domestic and imported beer. Also, they had a compliment of fine liquor, wine, and champagne. If you wanted to have a party, you went to John's. Religiously, they checked I.Ds. My fake I.D. from Michigan had not yet made it to the fake I.D. book they kept near the register. I guess I did look 23 or so when I was 18. Acquiring money for these purchases was no problem, either.

We collected 5 dollars from every guy on the floor. We easily had over $200 to buy alcohol. In the late 80's that was a lot of money for such a purpose. I can remember starting off one party with 20 cases of beer and a car trunk load of liquor. That was enough to get us started- but not enough to finish.

We charged guys $3 and girls $2. The stream of people was constant. Easily, we made $200 dollars for 3 straight hours. After several trips to Johns, we ended up with over 70 cases of beer and enough liquor to take the paint off of a semi-truck. It was at one of those parties that I earned the aforementioned nickname: "Sugar".

People would come to our parties before they went to the bars, after they came from the bars, or in place of the bars. After things started to clear out at around 1 or 2 in the morning, a couple of guys turned up- seemingly looking for trouble. They were drunk. I was drunk. Most of the people milling around were drunk. This was not the recipe for good conflict resolution.

They were complaining that there were no hot women left and they wanted their money back. I didn't like the way they were badmouthing our party. I subsequently went into my crazy Negro routine. This was very effective in the state of Iowa. Hollering, cussing, and throwing stuff scared the hell out of people. It was like they were watching J.J. from Good Times or Erkel from Family Matters mixed with Mr. T. from the A-Team. To calm me down some sober individual gave the guys back their money and they left.

They called me Sugar after the boxer, Sugar Ray Leonard. My antics must have been very shocking because not one punch was even thrown. Alcohol made my antics outlandish and my behavior dangerous.

Getting drunk and hooking up with women was the college way. It was the Burge way. Burge Hall had a national reputation for wild, drunken craziness. Playboy magazine called Burge "the Party Education Center." David Letterman had Burge ranked #3 as the best dorm to party in. It was also known nationally for a place to easily have sex. That it was.

I found that out early in my freshman year at a party on another floor in Burge. This was a female wing. It didn't take long for me to find a woman who was as wasted as I. Luckily, she also enjoyed my antics. When I went to her room, I made sure to close the blinds. My behavior made my life as a student at the University of Iowa impossible. My grades suffered miserably.

I partied myself out of school. At one point during my freshman year, I went out drinking Tuesday through Sunday. My roommates wondered where I got the money from to fund that destructive behavior. Whether good or bad, we can always find ways to do what we want. The fact that I was smart meant little.

My time was consumed by consumption. It was a feeble attempt to escape the person that I thought I was.

My first GPA was 1.00. That was a "D" average. I had never performed so academically low in my life. I even performed better at Cass Tech. I was put on academic probation. My behavior didn't change. I continued to drink, party, and be an overall poor student.

My second semester I earned a 1.66. That was better, but still dismal. Even worse was the fact that the minimum freshman grade point average was 1.6 back in those days. I wasn't ready for what was about to happen. I can remember that day like it was today. It was Cass Tech all over again.

I opened the letter telling me that I was not allowed to register for 2 consecutive semesters. Those letters never read: "You flunked out" but they might as well have. Failing my family, friends, and most importantly myself- I was devastated. Sitting there in my house at the kitchen table in Detroit- Iowa City and my drunken foolishness in Burge Hall had come to pay me a visit. That letter had invisible ink that read: "You reap what you sow, you get what you give, and you did it to yourself." There was a sliver of hope however; an appeal process.

My appeal letter must have been as convincing as my crazy Negro routine. I was readmitted on academic probation. My academic performance was not convincing my 3rd semester either. Even though I earned a paltry 1.88 it was higher than the minimum I needed. But, it was not high enough to raise my accumulative GPA from the grave. So, I flunked out of the University of Iowa for the second time.

Chapter 14
THE AWAKENING

John 11:43-44 He cried with a loud voice, "Lazarus, come forth!' And he who had died came out bound hand and foot with graveclothes…

My awakening would not be so dramatic. I was like a good used car that still had a lot of miles left. My battery was dead. I needed a jump. Time would be necessary to get me to operating fully. Not days, weeks, or months, but years would transpire before all of my major repairs would be finished. Like that used car, I would need a tune-up, to replace my cracked windshield, get new tires, and make sure all my instruments were in working order. Without this; I would not be nimble. These damages were caused by others and perhaps more unfortunately by my own doing. However, if I wanted a smooth ride, I was responsible for fixing it all myself.

Shame was my only friend as I returned home to Detroit after flunking out. I was 19 years old, broke, with no car, and had no idea what I was going to do. Since I lived in the bluest collar town in America, I figured I should get a job. With no skills or training, my options were limited. My buddy Brian's mom had a friend with a solution.

Ms. Hill's best girlfriend, Elaine, worked for a retail store called Colonial Merchandise Mart located in downtown Detroit on Griswold Ave. It sold toys, small appliances, and other gift items. She got me a job. That would be my place of employment while I served out my one year expulsion from America's best university. I would earn a whopping $3.55 an hour.

There were actually two locations. Separated by one city block on Griswold, you could communicate store- to-store with two cans connected by string. "Aunt" Elaine worked at one store and I was to work at the other. It seemed like a good hook up. "The best laid plans often go awry."

The manager of the store where I was to work wanted to get one of her relatives a job. She was denied by the owner. Elaine was not. That's how I got the job without having to fill out an application. So, here I come all bright-eyed and bushy tailed. This knowledge was all but unbeknownst to me at the time.

On my first day of work, I was ordered to wash the store's windows inside and out. I was getting schooled in office politics 101, it seemed. It appeared that there was an axe to grind. Unfortunately, it was on my neck. We actually had a window washer that came regularly. It was that type of situation.

Elaine complained and got the lady to lighten up on me a bit. Her disposition towards me would vary between mild indifference to outright contempt during my time there. Both were an improvement. It wasn't long before I started to realize that I had put myself in that predicament. If I were still in college, I never would have been treated poorly by this woman. She wasn't the problem- I was. My windows and mirrors were replaced first. I could now see more clearly.

GRADUATE

Detroit is made sort of like a bicycle wheel. Downtown is the hub. Streets like Jefferson, Woodward, Grand River, and Michigan all start Downtown. Michigan Avenue was a trail used for trading back in the frontier days. It connects the downtowns of Detroit and Chicago. Gratiot Avenue is another of these streets that connects to the hub. It happens to cross Rohns Street.

Since I didn't have a car, I rode the Gratiot bus to work every day. These could be the most eventful 30 minute slots of a person's life. You might see teenagers kissing on the back of the bus. Sometimes, self-proclaimed preachers would get on the bus-reciting their favorite bible verses. Before the cell phone people talked to each other about a range of topics. Many times, they were as insightful as the six o'clock news. The event that woke me up had no words at all.

There is a saying, "The eyes are the window to the soul." Riding to work one morning, I looked deeply into the eyes of the people on the bus. Their eyes were lifeless. It's like the joy, hope, and energy had been sucked right out of them. They looked like the walking dead, just going through the motions of everyday life. Whether day or night, morning or afternoon, they seemed to be awaiting the Angel of Death to set them free. It was tragic.

That day, I made a vow to myself. I wanted to find out what did this to scores of Black people. In some way I knew that what had happened to them was connected to what was happening inside of me. I wanted to help by attempting to undo what had been done. I wanted to fix it like a mechanic. Doing so; I knew I would be helping myself in the process simultaneously. For the first time, my life had purpose. This purpose was the jumpstart. Just like a car, it could have a working engine, but still major and minor repairs.

Up until that point, I had not seen many functional romantic relationships between a man and a woman. My father had five children by three different women. Bib was my grandmother's live-in boyfriend who would leave us high and dry. Rohns Street provided very little in this area as well. There were husbands and wives, but not enough for me to learn from. As a matter of fact, the Hood in general praised the "ladies man" type. Women were looked at as possessions; and the more possessions the better.

I've often heard that a man and a woman are halves that come together in a relationship to make a whole. That is not true. Only whole people can come together to make a healthy, functional, and complete relationship. Rarely is that the case. No one is perfect. Yet, there is a level of healthy self-esteem, self-confidence, and respect a person must have when they look in the mirror. If they do not have that for themselves, how can they have that for another? If you cannot love yourself, how can you expect to love somebody else? Needless to say, my first real relationship was destined for the junkyard.

Amber was the first in a lengthy line of failed relationships. Through them, I would learn about women, but most importantly I would learn about myself. Starting with her, I would come to learn about my fears, my insecurities, and my immaturity. She was a necessary part in my life's development. This relationship would later help me make repairs to myself.

Colonial Merchandise Mart, where I worked, was located downtown. Many of the public buses that serviced the Westside of the city started and ended their routes in Cadillac Square. This was a small park right outside of where I worked. I would see buses filled with people loading and unloading all day whilst I was at work.

GRADUATE

Amber rode the Grand River bus to Cass Tech mostly every day. That was not a problem when you were coming. She would get off at a stop a block or so away from the school. Trying to catch the Grand River afterschool going in the other direction was virtually impossible though. The bus would be packed with adults getting off of work and school kids who went to Eastside schools. Many Cass Tech students walked the mile or so downtown to get on the bus at the beginning of the route. It was not long before the bloodhound in me would sniff her out among the crowds.

We started by hanging out downtown. Wandering from bus stop to bus stop holding hands, hugging, and kissing- it was our routine. Young love birds with no nest. It would not be long until we found one.

Amber's mother worked the graveyard shift. That was our opportunity. I would come over and spend the night several times a week. Sometimes, I would hover in the shadows like a ghost until I saw her mother get into her car and leave. Finding mutual activities at that time of night was seldom difficult.

My parents never knew that I had gotten Amber pregnant. This was twice in three years that I had managed my part in conception. I had no idea of the gravity of my behavior. My toy store pay was not enough to buy a car; let alone raise a child. Her mother took her to get an abortion so fast our heads span. Clearly, her mom was not ready for grandchildren. Likewise, we were not ready to become parents. I was 19 and she was only 16.

At that time, I thought the necessary ingredient for a relationship was attraction. Opportunity was the only necessary component for sex. There is more to it than that, of course. I was careless and foolish. I was now operational; but still needing serious repairs. My girlfriend was no better.

Amber did not have a relationship with her father from what I could tell. She had also tragically experienced the death of a younger sibling. The worst part was that she was younger than I. We both needed to be on some therapist's chaise longue. We settled for her bed. We walked hand in hand happily off of a cliff together.

Two broken people in a relationship was a bad combination. We both lacked healthy self-esteem and self-confidence. It was not long before she cheated on me and I cheated on her too. Respect was nowhere to be found. It was like I was dating myself. To some degree, I was. Perhaps that's what brought us together.

I believe we attract people into our lives. Whole people attract whole people. Broken people attract broken people. At that point in my life, I was attracted to people who were seriously flawed like I was. That would be the case for many years. One thing is for certain. Having healthy romantic relationship is important to success. If left untamed, these relationships can have far reaching effects into every area of a person's life; including their academic life.

My year of exile from the hallowed halls of the University of Iowa ended. I had learned plenty in Detroit. There was more to learn in Iowa City. It was time shake off my grave clothes.

Chapter 15

G.K., LAMES LEE, AND THE AFRO HOUSE

Every great achiever is inspired by a great mentor – Lailah Gifty Akita

The African American Cultural Center was a place where students, mostly black, came to hang out. It was a converted home that had been redecorated like a student center. It had a small library, a computer, and a television with cable. That latter part was important because cable was a luxury that most of us could not afford in those days. The Afro House even had a kitchen complete with a sink, stove, and refrigerator. It was a home away from home for many of us.

The Black Student Union meetings were held there mostly every week. Sometimes, we would watch sporting events upstairs on the T.V. Several Black Greek organizations would use the basement for their "meetings" as well. If there was a lenient employee on staff at the center; we would use it for parties and after sets. This was totally against university policy, of course. A few times when there was no one to let us in for these impromptu gatherings, someone would climb in a window and open up the door. It was usually a student from Chicago. They were good at that sort of thing. We knew nothing about those shady behaviors in Detroit.

This is where I met two guys who would help me by example. They were passionate about the Black experience. Political, opinionated, and driven were the characteristics they both shared. James Lee was tall and resolute like Brother Malcolm. I saw him get into a confrontation with a young White coed at a rally and he said to him: "Are you ready to die right now? Because I am!" In that moment he probably was. The other student deflated like a balloon with a small puncture.

Greg Kelley, often called G.K., was smooth like Dr. Martin Luther King Jr. In many ways he was the ying to James Lee's yang. They sort of balanced each other out. He was born and raised in slain Black Panthers activist territory- Fred Hampton's stomping grounds of Maywood, Illinois right outside of Chicago. Greg was smart, dapper, and good-looking. He introduced me to a book by Cornell West called "Race Matters". What I needed at the time to figure out the great race question- I found in these two brothers.

When I returned to school, my best friend from home Brian Hill (B-Hill for short) was ending his third semester at Iowa. We had seen and done so much back in Detroit together, he knew me as well as anyone could. We met playing football on a vacant lot around the corner from Rohns Street and became as tight as 10 toes in one sock. We had known each other for almost10 years before we even knew Iowa City existed.

We met up with James Lee, G.K., and some others to watch the Cosby Show in the Afro House once a week. We debated, laughed, and pondered the greatest questions that our exploding young minds could fathom over a bucket of Kentucky Fried Chicken. We often joked about the irony of Black students eating KFC in the Afro House on a predominately white campus. They helped give me life. We helped give each other life.

James was the president of the Black Student Union and G.K. was the vice-president. They understood the university better than I did when I returned in my hunger for knowledge. There was an annual meeting for students that rotated around the Big Eight Conference schools (now the Big 12 Conference.) It was called the Big 8 Black Student Leadership Conference. Brian and I were invited to go over a chicken leg, coleslaw, and a few laughs.

That year, the conference was held at Iowa State University. It was only a 90 minute drive away. The conference consisted of seminars during the day and parties at night. That was my kind of mix! Big 8 was the first time I heard a civil and women's rights activist, Sonia Sanchez, speak. She was insightful, inspirational, and thought-provoking. Speakers like her helped me to understand the problem I first recognized on a Detroit bus.

Nighttime was filled with parties and chasing cute college girls. Of the latter, I was quite proficient. James Lee would find that out as well as anyone one evening. The university had paid for only one room. It was B Hill, G.K., James Lee and I sharing two queen size beds. James was already asleep by the time we made it back to the room with a few girls. I slipped my new friend into the bed where James was sleeping. At some point she made a certain noise that woke up James. He looked relieved that I was not by myself.

These guys were more to me than just a bunch of laughs. They served as a guide post, a traffic light, and a roadmap of where I still had to go. They were mentors in the purest sense. Every student needed at least one. I needed several.

Their mentorship to me was unplanned, unscripted, but unmistakable. I needed those older guys to help me get on track at Iowa. They did just that by example. I was never sat down and taught the ways of college life like a father might do with his son. Through our association- I learned and tried to keep step. I would go on to become Black Student Union president like both of them. I would go on to graduate like both of them. I would go on to live a life of purpose, like both of them.

After they graduated, I was well on my way to earning my degree. They were not my first mentors, and certainly not my last. It would be wise for a person to have a mentor for each stage of their life. It's like having a living, breathing roadmap. Immeasurable was their influence on my fragile college path at that time.

I was asked to speak on a black alumni panel in Iowa City many years after my undergraduate years. I mentioned how much G.K. had meant to me. He was as surprised as many of my other friends from college. Never underestimate the influence you have on people in your life. People are watching. You may be the only thing that keeps them on the right track. That's good for them as well as for you.

Chapter 16
BLACK HAWK DOWN

Defeating racism, tribalism, intolerance, and all forms of discrimination will liberate us all, victim and perpetrator alike. – Ban Ki-Moon

Cambus was the student-run transit system at the University of Iowa. Buses crisscrossed campus giving students access to all parts of the area. Some routes even went off campus to nearby student housing. There was a bus and van that operated early into the morning on the weekends. It was called the "Drunk Bus" because it provided a safe ride home to bar goers. I rode it home many times.

Riding the yellow and black buses could be like sharing a tin can with a bunch of sardines. The buses became packed in between 8 a.m. and noon. Standing students heading to morning classes would move like a bobble-head on a car dashboard as the buses navigated the campus streets. Seats were a premium commodity at these times. That's what I thought.

My first experiences on these buses started my education in Black Hawk Down. Time after time, I would sit on a jam-packed, standing-room-only bus with a vacant seat next to me. It took several trips for me to even notice what was going on. Initially, I thought I was spilling over on to the next seat in some way. So, I would contort myself like a circus clown entering a tiny car to make sure I wasn't in anyone's way.

That was not it. People still choose to stand the majority of the time. After a while I got defiant and placed my book bag in the open seat; sprawling out like I was at home watching TV. I must have looked as weird; I was contorted like Bozo the Clown. Something was wrong; I knew I was not crazy. It became a frustrating, isolating, and dehumanizing fact of life in Iowa for me. Soon I would learn that I was not alone.

Many African-American students would meet up at the IMU, Iowa Memorial Union, to hang out before, after, and sometimes during class. Since many of us were from big cities like Chicago, St. Louis, or Detroit, we were sharing stories of our culture shock. It was there that I realized we all had something in common.

In frustration, I mentioned how no one would sit next to me on the Cambus. When I mentioned that, it was like a heavy load had been lifted off a bunch of chocolate chests. "That happens to me too!" a girl said. "Me too" one of the guys said. Other students sat in reflection. You could see a light bulb flick on when they realized the same thing was happening to all of them. It was like someone was telling us a big secret.

Knowing that I was sharing this experience with another group of people held a great sense of relief. It did not seem as bad because I knew then that it was not personal. I was starting to become concerned that I had a body odor problem. My low self-esteem magnified events like this. Everything seemed worse. Some White fraternity guys were racially insensitive.

Whether it was at Halloween, in some parade, or at a dramatic production- white frat boys would dress up in black face. I mean the full Al Jolson, Mamie, shoe polish on the face deal. Also, they would wear afro wigs, sweat pants, and other clothing to represent themselves as African-American. It was absurd. When confronted, they rarely saw anything wrong with their behavior. It was so disrespectful and they didn't even seem to acknowledge it.

I do not want to characterize all white fraternity men as the perpetrators of this offensive deed. Other white guys would exhibit this behavior. More brazen were the frat guys though. This is something that was not limited to the University of Iowa campus; but was nationwide phenomenon. On some campus around the country this type of thing would make local or national news. Black Hawk Down made me the black spokesmen on many occasions.

Rarely was I in a discussion class with other African-Americans. On a campus that was 8% Black in a state that was less than 2% Black this was sure to be the case. Unfortunately, many of us were forced with being the mouthpiece for the whole race. That was a tall order for an 18 year-old.

Often classroom discussion would turn to something dealing with the African-American experience. When that would happen, everyone including the professor, in some cases, would look directly at me. In a split second, I had been Jesse Jacksoned; I was forced to speak for all dark-skinned people when I barely knew myself. The pressure was immense. On cue I would have to come up with something relatively sensible. That was not easy for a guy with a self-confidence problem. Sometimes things got dangerous on campus.

Johnson Avenue's tree-lined street would be very dark in spots. Over by the business building was a parking structure. I was walking on the other side instead of taking the drunk bus home. In the distance, I could see a shadowy figure approaching me. In between the trees, light from the street lamps would poke through. As this figure got closer, I could tell it was a white guy. Next, my ears detected something strange.

As he walked within a few steps of me, I heard a clicking sound. Staggering by, I recognized the sound but could not quite figure out what it was. After he walked by me a few steps I heard the sound again. At the time, I could not place where I had heard that noise.

For weeks, my mind struggled to identify that sound. One day, like fog had been lifted, I realized what that sound was. I would bet a dollar to a dime that it was a pocket knife being opened and closed. That distinctive clicking sound was very familiar to me. I guess living in Iowa City for so long had taken that identification from my conscious mind and stored it in the reservoirs of my subconscious.

Of course, I could be wrong. I never saw the knife. Nor can I be sure that it had anything to do with my race. The guy could have just been afraid of whoever was coming toward him on that dark lonely street. I did fit the description of "the Prowler." At that time in my life, I was only threatening to a bottle of Jack Daniels. Besides, that clicking noise could have been a gun. Black Hawk Down came to Burge Hall.

One night in my freshman year while living in Burge Hall, Chris and Bryce (my roommates) and I were a little stir-crazy. None of us was able to sleep. We laughed, giggled, and talked for over an hour with the lights off for bed. We decided to share our insomnia with our neighbors next door. So, Bryce and

Chris pounded on the wall to wake them up. It was juvenile and immature, but funny. After about 5 minutes of that, we heard some loud pounding back. We gathered it meant you better stop because we are getting angry. They stopped. I never pounded on the wall, but that was not the deduction. My guilt was already certain.

Doug, Tony, and Larry were our next door neighbors. They happened to be White. As a group, they were good-humored, light-hearted, and fun-loving bunch like most college kids. One of them would then say something to me that I had not heard before, nor have I heard since. It shook me to my core.

Firstly, Larry assumed that it was me who had done the pounding. Why I do not know. These are his exact words. "The next time you decide to knock on someone's wall you should remember that I know people in high places in the Ku Klux Klan and the life you save may be your own." I was stunned into silence. I cannot remember who was around or where we were. That part is a blur. What I do remember is the sense of isolation, helplessness, and fear that immediately arrested me. What came next was worse.

The Spring Break was approaching. I was homesick and really wanted to go home. I cried and begged my parents to foot the bill for my transportation back to Detroit. We were poor. They couldn't afford it. I spent my first Spring Break in college at Burge Hall.

The massive dormitory was virtually deserted. There were maybe 10 people in the entire building. Knowing that I was virtually alone caused me much distress. I was terrified those few days over the break. Fear had me in a choke hold.

We had communal showers; there was a large room with a bunch of spigots coming out of the wall. I can remember being in the shower and hearing some noises. My mind shot back to Larry's comments. I was sure someone was coming to harm me. Fear consumed me like a wild fire. Every little noise caused my heart to race. Larry was oblivious to the magnitude of his comment.

Months later I worked up the courage to ask Larry about his comments. He acted as if he did not even remember what he said. He added that he wondered why I had not been speaking to him. Was he serious? Could a person be that clueless? I don't think so. I truly believe that he was embarrassed that I had confronted him about the racial threat in front of our peers. Black Hawk Down, my education in race relations, was not all bad.

Blair was more than beautiful. She was one of the prettiest women that I had met at the University of Iowa. The fact that she was White had nothing to do with the matter. Moreover, she was a dancer. Not that she could dance; but she was trained in ballet and modern forms of dance. She had that toned and tight dancer's body. The most important feature about Blair was that she was totally in to me. It was evident from the beginning.

One of my professors, Dr. Woodard, was contemplating producing a play that called for actors and dancers. We all met at a studio and ran through some lines in the script. She twirled around like something out of a dream. I was impressed by her poise and grace. It was evident that she was special. The cast exchanged numbers so that we might practice together outside of studio time.

Blair called me several times. I could hear the interest in her voice. At the least, she wanted me to ask her out. Yet I never did. I was afraid. The idea of interracial dating made me uncomfortable. My ignorance held me back. Guys do stupid things.

Blair was not the kind to be denied. She called me and asked me to come to her apartment. I knew what was coming. When I arrived no one was there but us. We practiced over our lines for about 5 minutes before we started kissing. Needless to say, she was a great dancer. The following weeks would teach me something about myself.

Blair and I would meet to eat, practice our lines, and hang out. I came to her place. She came to mine. One day she suggested that we hang out at the Rez. It was like a beach in the middle of Iowa. It was very public. I was not.

My response to that suggestion doused whatever fire Blair had burning for me. I was not sure how people would respond to an interracial couple in public. She responded by not taking my calls. That was that.

When I saw her at one of the local bars, I tried to correct my mistake. I told her we could go anywhere and do anything. It was too late. The tears that I saw in her eyes confirmed that. I realized in a flash that I had done to her what others had done to me. I allowed race to cloud my judgment. I never saw Blair again. Something was suddenly abundantly clear to me.

Being a Black student at a white majority university was extremely difficult at times. My self-esteem and self-confidence did not make things any better. If I was to get all my repairs done, I would have to come to some resolution on race-related matters. My minority status could have been a lifelong struggle within itself. As fate would have it, I was going to get another side to the race issue.

During the end of my time at Iowa, I had really figured things out. Classes were not boring anymore. They did not seem like a necessary evil. I did not count sheep in them. Fully engaged in the educational process, I focused my attention. I became well organized, managed my time, and shrank my circle of friends- but I still had one major issue.

Because I screwed up so badly during my earlier years, my financial aid package decreased significantly. Poor grades and mismanagement of money led to a huge bill at the end of one semester. I was in a serious hole. $5,000 dollars for a college student seemed like a million bucks when you're working $7 an hour jobs. I had to sit out of school for a year and a half just to pay off a fraction of that bill earlier. I was in a dire financial situation.

I was at the point where I thought I would have to hang my head in shame again and return home. Options were limited. I reasoned that being at home would cut my expenses and allow me to pay off the money I owed to the university faster. That made sense. I let my boss know at work what my issue was and what I had decided to do. What happened next was truly amazing.

Arlene was a petite, kind-hearted, and understanding woman. The fact that she was white made no difference to me. After hearing my situation, she said plainly: "Really? Let me talk to my husband because he has money." I was thinking to myself: "I did tell you I needed $5,000 dollars didn't I?" That would not matter. I had not met her husband John yet.

They invited me and a friend over for dinner to discuss the matter further. As I walked around their palatial home, I saw pictures of her husband in Alaska, Africa, Australia, and other exotic locations. Dead stuffed heads of unfortunate moose, elk, bears, and lions stared at me as I gazed up at them. His hobby was big game hunting. That is not a poor man's sport.

He had worked for a small company in Iowa. Being an engineer, he worked to perfect the technology for a little known appliance back in the 50's and 60's. It had the potential to be revolutionary. The company was Amana and the appliance was called the microwave oven. You may have heard of it. Arlene was right. Her husband did have money.

At the end of dinner, we sat at the kitchen table enjoying some coffee and conversation. He directly asked; "Are you going to pay this money back?" I responded- "Yes." He wrote me a check for $5,000 and that was that. I was astonished.

I paid the money back in a couple of months, graduated in a year, and had learned enough about race to live the rest of my life. Arlene and her husband John were white as the driven snow. I soon learned that race meant little to good, caring, and compassionate people. The world is filled with Larrys and Johns. Each one should be judged "by the content of their character and not the color of their skin." This was a vital lesson to learn if I were to continue to repair myself.

My English courses were fertile ground for my developing understanding of race. Classes like Literature and the Culture of America After 1800, Selected American Authors, and 20th Century Literature were fascinating. Yet, these classes usually lacked a certain perspective.

"Why isn't there any Black authors being read in this class," I asked with a semi-dramatic puzzled look on my face? Students froze. The professor reddened. I expanded. "Isn't this a selected American author's class?" I continued. "Why weren't there any black authors selected?" I said emphasizing the word selected. He had no sensible answer. Even though caught off-guard and a bit embarrassed; I could tell he appreciated the question. He would become one of my favorite professors. I took two more classes with him. He would go on to help me graduate.

It was not enough for me to just think of myself. I had to be concerned with people that had no voice. Those people that lived without spunk or purpose were always on my mind. They needed an advocate. I was becoming a mechanic of sorts. I desired to fix problems that I saw in racial matters, gender equality, and fairness. Social justice was the goal.

Chapter 17
GRADUATION TIME

You are educated. Your certification is in your degree. You may think of it as the ticket to the good life. Let me ask you to think of an alternative. Think of it as your ticket to change the world.
– Tom Brokaw

Senioritis is a disorder experienced by students who are about to graduate from an academic institution. One suffers from tiredness, restlessness, and overall laziness. I was infected about two months before I was to graduate from Iowa. I was such a good student now, that I could coast and still earn A's and B's in all my classes. It had been a long undergraduate process and I was worn out. It took me 10 years to get a 4 year degree. Womanizing had lost its appeal. Drinking occurred every so often. Lounging was my main activity.

I lived in a lackluster studio apartment. It was in the basement of a house two blocks from campus. It must have been near the water level because it was always humid and sort of damp. Centipedes, water bugs, and other creepy crawlies often raced across my floor or wall. It seemed like they were making a mad dash for freedom from some eternal jail known as my bedroom. At that point, I did not care where I lived. My focus was laser tight. Graduation was my only priority. I had made it to the finish line.

Besides, I knew something was up when the landlord cut me a great deal on the rent. He usually wore tight jeans, a neck full of gold chains, and a perm like Tina Turner in the 70's. "This house is not zoned for another residential space," he said. He continued, "But, you can stay down here and just look out for the zoning inspector." Good deal, I thought. When the lady would stumble down the basement stairs and knock on the door, I would mute the TV and take a nap. It worked every time I thought. The zoning commission contacted the owner to request an inside inspection of the property. He and I spent a whole day piling all my stuff in the furnace room. Even the water bugs were pissed.

When the coast was clear, I spent most of my time down there sleeping and looking at BET (Black Entertainment Network). Back then in Iowa City, it was not shown for 24 hours. It would play for half the day and sometimes switch to another station right in the middle of programming.

One afternoon, I was watching BET and reading Ebony magazine. This color architectural drawing I was looking at was amazing. It had a large dome and two massive African masks hanging over the door. "Charles H. Wright Museum of African American History" the article read. I was excited that it was going to be built in my hometown of Detroit. A strange feeling swept over me like the warming rays of sunlight. Inspiration was on the horizon.

As I walked across the Pentacrest (Five buildings that use to serve as the state capital buildings now used by the university for classroom and office space) down the hill to the IMU, I had an epiphany. I think. It was like a sort of enlightenment, a revealing, like someone was telling me a secret. It was as clear as day.

You are going to be a teacher. "A teacher?" I thought. "I am in my last semester of school!" Graduation was right around the corner. What idiot changes their major right before graduation? I pondered the thought from what I understood of teaching at the time. I thought about taking classes in the college of education. Trying to get an education degree would add 18 months on to my already 10 year college career. No way, I thought. I stuck to the plan in place.

This revelation would be one of the most important of my life. At the time I did not understand totally what it meant. Teacher was intended to mean educator. It would take time and more growth for me to grasp the scope of my purpose. I saw the trees, but not the forest. How better to fix others and myself- than to become an educator? Peter F Drucker said, "No one learns as much about a subject as one who is forced to teach it." I was not forced. I was led.

The night before graduation, several of my friends drove from Detroit to see me walk across the stage at Carver Hawkeye Arena. Reggie Harper, his brother Claude Harper, and another friend Deon Teart had driven over seven hours to support me on my special day. That really meant a lot to me because not one member of my family had ever set foot on the campus of the University of Iowa. Those guys were my family. I had to take them to my old stomping grounds: Downtown Iowa City and the myriad of bars. The prodigal son was back for one last pitcher of beer.

We settled on the upstairs of the Airliner. It was right across the street from the Pentacrest. You could see it from the windows. What a great way to spend my last night as a student.

You would very rarely see football players out at that time of year. December graduations clashed with bowl game preparations. Nevertheless, one of the most thrilling players of recent Iowa football history, Tim Dwight, was celebrating too. He would go on to run a kick off back in the Superbowl the next season as he had done so many times in the Nile Kinnick football stadium on campus. He would go on to have a long career in the NFL. We chatted a bit and enjoyed a night with friends and family.

The next morning we headed to Carver Hawkeye Arena where basketball, volleyball, and wrestling matches were held. I was not in the stands like I had been so many times watching my friends play against the Big Ten's best teams, but I was seated on the floor. I, along with several hundred of my closest friends, was taking the court. There were a lot of dreams coming true that day. Hard work, late nights, and empty bank accounts were paying off on that crisp Saturday morning in Iowa City, Iowa.

In retrospect, I recognize that what helped me to become successful in high school were the same things that worked for me in college. There were people throughout my college career who helped me. I found several places where I could focus on studying. My circle of friends was those who were headed in the same direction as me. If you were not focused on graduation, you got little of my time. During my Iowa years, I found my purpose and was energized with passion. My 'what' and 'why' were answered for me. It was up to me now to find the 'how'.

For me, it had been a long 10 years since I graduated from high school. I made every possible mistake an undergraduate could make and still made it to graduation. I was not the same person who had walked on Iowa's campus looking like the mascot, Herky the Hawk. I had grown, matured, and evolved in to someone much better than I was before. The finished product- I was not. Triumphant and on my way- I certainly was.

Chapter 18

THE W(RIGHT) MUSEUM

"The purpose of life is to contribute in some way to making things better" – Robert F. Kennedy

"I have my degree in African-American World Studies" I said confidently. "We don't have any openings at this time" the woman responded. I was not deterred. Nothing was going to stop me from getting a job at that place. My persistence led me to call back many times. I could not and would not give up. Sometimes, you have to be a nuisance to get what you want. In this case I was just that.

Being fresh home from college, I was working at an optometrists' office. That was not my calling in life. I knew that, but it paid. I needed to see this place that I first saw from the pages of Ebony magazine in my Honeycomb Hideout in Iowa City in person. There was a play being performed in the theatre there: Lorraine Hansberry's "A Raisin in the Sun". That was my opportunity. Walter Lee Younger and I were old friends.

The building was grand. It looked even more impressive as it jumped off the pages of my mind and into the massive structure that lay in front of me. There were two main entrances.

Three sets of imposing ten-foot bronze doors invited guests inside. Until they were redesigned they were as heavy as the doors on an armored truck.

Over the doors, attached to the top of the structure were two huge black and gold metal African masks. They must have been over 10 feet as well. Inspired by Western African peoples- they set the mood for what was inside.

The interior of the building was just as splendid as on the outside. The sun shined bright through the huge doomed glass roof. Coming down from the ceiling were large cement pillars that had a rope design. Every facet of the opulent design was related to people of African ancestry.

Walking up the stairs of the Warren Avenue entrance- guests enter into the Ford Rotunda sponsored by the Ford Motor Company. This circular space was a huge meeting place. It was rented out on occasions for weddings, galas, and other special events. The design produced strange acoustics. You could hear a couple whispering on the other side of the circular room like they were standing right next to you. This was not the place to relay secrets. The eyes beckoned up to see the flags around the circumference of the ceiling from everywhere a person of African descent lives- the African Diaspora.

Hubert Massey's terrazzo masterpiece, called Genealogy, was embedded in the floor of the rotunda. There, one sees the African experience showcased with wonderful artistic expression. Seeing this work of art from the heights of the offices on the mezzanine makes its beauty even more profound.

Adinkra symbols (from Ghana) were carved into most of the woodwork on doors and the visitors' desk. Each symbol had its own special meaning. One had two lizards intersecting so that they share the same stomach. It emphasizes the importance of unity, community, and harmony. Another symbol is called Hwemudua, "Measuring Stick", it stresses the need to strive for excellence in all things. All this I experienced on my first visit to the museum.

When I walked through the doors, I felt a warm feeling. It was like I drove through a car wash with the water and hot wax oozing down onto me. It was familiar and refreshing. I immediately knew this would be a special place for me. My expectations would be exceeded. Now I know it was destiny, purpose, and opportunity all coming together at the same time.

Dr. Charles H. Wright, an Ob-Gyn, started collecting African artifacts and memorabilia in the basement of his home. He was inspired by a WWII museum he visited in Denmark. Dr. Wright believed that there should be a place that celebrated the achievements and contributions of Black people. In 1965, with the help of others, he would open the Afro-American Museum of Detroit. It evolved into the building that I stood in. I would spend 5 years of my life working at the Wright Museum, as it's called today. It was there that I learned that I had been given a great talent. I would work with several very talented, capable, and passionate individuals.

Robert Norwood, affectionately called Chief, was in charge of the security for the Wright. Doing so was no easy job. The building itself was the size of an automotive plant. During the summer months, people would be in virtually each one of the 125,000 square feet. Visitors from family reunions would pack the museum to capacity. He managed a staff of guards with professionalism, courtesy, and excellence. Due to financial reasons, he was laid off. His plight was inevitably the same for many other great employees at the museum.

KB, Keisha Bell, worked in the museum store during college. She would later go on to become the store's manager. She supervised staff, bought merchandise, and balanced the books. Her hard work and effort made the store as profitable as it had ever been. She was laid off too. Following the death of my grandmother; KB helped me stumble along until I was able to get my footing. Some employees left the museum to much success.

Toya Hankins did special programs at the museum. Her main function was planning, managing, and supervising the African World Festival. This was a three day outdoor event that would see about a million visitors by the end of the weekend. During our time, it was held at Hart Plaza in downtown Detroit. After she left, Toya became the manager for R&B singer KEM, and others.

I landed a job in no other than the Education Department. My official title was Museum Teacher. We were entrusted with creating programs for museum exhibits, curriculum for school age visitors, and providing guided tours of the galleries. I did not need a degree in education anymore because I was getting on-the-job training. It's interesting how things can work themselves out when you're willing to answer the call of your purpose. You just have to be prepared to take the first step.

Usually, it took museum teachers about a month of training before they felt comfortable enough to do a tour without any help. Three days after I was hired, I did my first tour. It was clear to everyone, including myself, that I had a gift for speaking. Talking about the contributions, achievements, and participation of Black people in the world really fuelled me. I was able to take boring facts and craft them into dramatic, engaging, and inspirational stories. One day I was giving a tour and a woman started crying- I was shocked. She was just overwhelmed by how

I told the stories of our ancestors. Also, at the end of tours, I would commonly be given handshakes that doubled as covert tips. Getting paid to talk, who would have believed that?

During the summertime the museum would be filled with family reunion groups. They were the most generous. Family love filled their hearts and loosened their wallets to my delight. On one particular tour, I received a nice tip. I had no idea that a writer from the local newspaper was in that group. Impressed, she wrote about the tour I gave her family in her column. (You can read the article on my website.)

My self-esteem and self-confidence soared. I was riding a high. Things were not perfect in my life, but they were getting much better. Passion and purpose changed the way I looked at myself and the world around me. Having the opportunity to sit down and read for hours about the heroism, intelligence, and flat-out grit of Black people was important for me. Knowing where I came from was essential for knowing where I was going. It's sometimes called the knowledge of self. This is an essential building block for healthy self-esteem and self-confidence.

V.I.P tours were a big deal. Often celebrities, politicians, and other notables came to the museum. On one day, the then-governor of Michigan, Jennifer Granholm, came for a special event. She was to get a tour. That day the museum teachers were to decide amongst themselves who would provide the tour. My colleagues hesitated and with my newfound confidence I stepped up quick. Things went very well. (See website for picture)

The University of Michigan rented the museum for a swanky event one evening. They had tables and chairs set up on the rotunda floor under the stars seen through the dome. Each chair was dressed in maize and blue with a big bow on the back. It looked like a weeding had come to the Wright. I was to do the tour that evening. When it was time, I started the tour. As I gave my introduction, which included where I graduated from, people started to laugh and snicker. I thought it was some type of Big Ten rivalry thing and shrugged it off. Graduating from the University of Iowa was a source of pride for me, of course.

When I did V.I.P tours I really tried to do a good job. It was like the more famous and bigger the audience, the better I performed. At the end of the tour, a small lady walked up from the back of the group. Her face was so familiar. She said, "Great job!" She was gushing a bit like a proud parent. She was the then-president of the University of Michigan, Mary Sue Coleman, and former president of the University of Iowa. We both transitioned from Iowa to Michigan. After the tour we chatted for a while. She ended with a great big 'keep up the good work." Educators always seek to inspire. Soon the walls of the museum could not contain me.

I got invited out by a former high school classmate to do a Black History program at his job. I was thrilled. They gave me a whopping $50. It was more than the tips at the museum. I was happy to have gas money for my car for the rest of week. My sights were too small at the time. They were not even set at all, really. I didn't have a clue what was about to happen. Things got better in a flash.

I did a tour for a group of about15 guys from Jacksonville, Florida at the museum. Afterwards, one of them, Bruce Terry Brown, approached me with an offer. He said that he was the president of the National Black Prosecutors Association and wanted me to speak at their national conference that was being held in Detroit the following summer. For some reason, I did not believe him. Clearly, I needed more repairs. I couldn't yet believe in myself… in my talent. He said I would be contacted by someone from the local chapter. I waited, apprehensively.

In about April, a woman called just like Bruce had said. She confirmed the date for my lecture. I was to speak at one of their receptions. The location was the GM Theatre of the Charles H. Wright Museum of African American History. I would be speaking at my job. It was a perfect set up for a perfect evening.

The talent and gifts I had been given as a speaker were on display there that night. It was like a flashpoint. All the skills I had developed and been blessed with, shined. My presentation was called: "What the History Books Forgot: African Contributions to World Civilization" (Go to my website to see a clip of that program). Afterwards, people raved about my program. They asked me for my business card. What business cards? "What business?" I thought. I was just speaking to people for gas money. Sometimes people see the good in us better than we do ourselves.

I exchanged contact information with several people that evening. Many were directors of government, state, and country agencies. After all was said and done; I would have spoken over 15 times from that one speech. Less than three weeks after that lecture, I was on a plane to Washington D.C. to speak for the Community Relations Service, part of the U.S. Department of Justice. I'm glad to say- they paid me more than gas money.

Ted McBurroughs was the director of FMS at the main building of the Department of Justice in Washington D.C. He asked me to present at their Black History Month program in February. I agreed. All of the arrangements had been made. His office called me in December. The speaker for their Martin Luther King Jr. program had cancelled out at the last minute. They asked me could I fill in. They offered me more money than for the Black History Month program. I agreed. The only problem was the mountain of paperwork. Since that honorarium amount exceeded a certain threshold- I had to register with the government's vendor system. Unknowingly, I had become a contractor for the government with the world's largest economy. That hassle has paid off several times over.

After the Martin Luther King Jr. Program in DC, a woman came up to me with an offer. "I'm interested in having you speak for our Black History month program at DEA (Drug Enforcement Agency) main," she said. I believed her. I was evolving. "How much do you charge?" she asked. I responded with my highest honorarium fee. She replied calmly: "Oh, we can afford that." Thankfully, that was not the end of the matter.

The woman from the DEA I met took a leave of absence. She referred me to another person. She sounded young like me. She asked me how much did I charge. That question led me to believe that the other woman had not told her the fee I had said. I was really honest. I said: "I'm not really sure what to charge?" She said: "Just charge 5." I thought 5? I said, "5?." She responded, "Yes, $5,000, we pay our speakers more than that- but that's a good place to get your foot in the door." I screamed when I hung up the phone. When purpose and passion meet opportunity- special things can happen.

At that lecture in the museum, two women, Reeva and Grace, came up to me and asked me to speak at their national conference. As soon as they opened their mouths- I was surprised. Their English accents delighted my ears. I hadn't spoken with someone from the United Kingdom before. Their organization was called the National Black Crown Prosecutors Association. They were from London, England. "Yeah Right!" I thought. There was no way that could happen. Truly believing in myself really took a while.

It had been about 5 years since I was lying around my apartment thumbing through Ebony magazine. Never in my wildest dreams could I have believed that my life would change so radically. But, the question needed to be asked- “Why not?” I had fought my way through college. I had vowed to help people. Now, most importantly, I had found that special talent that God has placed inside of all of us. It found me because I worked hard, I didn’t give up, and I was in the right place at the right time with the right skills and the right talents. Now, I was on my way from the New World to the Old World to experience only what I had dreamed about.

Chapter 19
JUMPING THE POND

Mind the gap! – unknown

"Is this your first time to England?" the airline attendant said as he scanned my ticket. "Yes" I replied. "You'll do well" he said with a devilish smile. Oh, I thought. He was talking about the ladies. He was not wrong. I was young, black, relatively good-looking, mostly well-dressed and had an American accent. I sparked a lot of interest just by simply opening my mouth. My self-confidence would improve greatly.

I was picked up at Gatwick Airport. Michael was a lean wiring type with a caramel complexion. He was a member of Grace and Reeva's organization and worked for the CPS, Crown Prosecutors Service. We took the train into London. Landmarks and recognizable streets whizzed by the train window. I was in a new world that seemed so familiar. My share of Sherlock Holmes movies and the like made this adventure on the other side of the pond as comfortable as going to the grocery store for milk. After we met up with Grace and Reeva, we headed to Liverpool- the birthplace of the Beatles. It seemed like a bit of a homecoming; since I was a big fan as a kid.

The conference hotel was located right on the docks in Liverpool. I could see ships sailing down the canal from my window. It was an amazing site. Everything was a learning experience. The baked beans at breakfast, the mayonnaise used as salad dressing, and the Queen's English were quite refreshing for me. Hundreds of years earlier- different kinds of ships sailed down that passageway outside of my window.

Working at the Wright, I had gained a love for museums. I made a habit of finding a good one in every city I visited. Liverpool was no exception. In walking distance from the hotel, I visited the International Slavery Museum on the 3rd floor of the Merseyside Maritime Museum. It was phenomenal.

The exhibition showed the ships that were made, the people that made them, and the depositing of Black Africans in and around Liverpool. The stories made my head spin. I was introduced to a whole new narrative of Black History. These things were not covered in my coursework for African-American World Studies at Iowa. These stories made the ships sailing past my hotel window seem much more significant.

My lecture at the conference went great. All in attendance were pleased. I had introduced my American style of public speaking to a UK audience. The content of Black History facts were new to a certain extent. Much of Black History in America is largely facts about African people in the New World. Black History in the UK is primarily about people of African descent from the Old World. It was great to open peoples' eyes like the Mariner's museum opened mine.

My trip to the UK was such a confidence booster. My self-esteem grew by leaps and bounds. Being the authority on Black Americans was a great position to hold. Informal conversations about the welfare of Black people and American politics were just as thrilling for me as it was for them. I would eventually travel to the UK many more times.

"You should come over" Grace said. The thought of leaving my problems behind for 10 days over the Christmas holiday was welcoming. Things were difficult at the time. The Wright was a non-profit organization that shared its financial status with its employees. I wasn't paid well. Slow times at the museum meant that our hours were cut to part-time. While my self-esteem was growing in one area; I still was struggling through my own personal Great Depression. Grace's invitation gave me a break from that reality.

Grace Ononiwu was a kind woman. Born in Nigeria, living as a UK citizen, she was doing quite well for herself. She was as stylish as she was smart. Gucci, Prada, and Cartier were all old friends of hers. She wore them well. Plus, she could cook like a gourmet chef. She was a testament to what hard work can do. Opening her home to me was exactly what I needed.

I was moody, depressed, and suffering from poverty. The flashes of brilliance in my public speaking career were not enough to totally raise my spirits. I had not learned the business well enough to boost my sagging income. That would take several more years. Grace had a great suggestion. I wasn't sold on it at first, though.

"Royce, you have a story," she said one evening. "A story?" I thought. In my mind it was similar to that of the Titanic. "You've been able to do some incredible things in your life. You should write a book about them." She continued. I still lacked some self-confidence and didn't feel that I had a story that people wanted to hear. At that time, I did not want to hear or live the story. My vision was still blurry. It was hard to see myself clearly in the mirror. The lack of money was clouding my judgment. She was right, though. It would take years for me to realize. Even in my state- I think I was able to help Grace as well.

She was dealing with some personal issues and was in the process of repairing herself. The process for her was mentally exhausting. "Royce, I'm tired" she said. She wanted to coast for a while and just enjoy the fruits of her labor. Opportunity rarely waits for coasting. It's here for a moment and then it closes its door like a bus and moves away to pick up passengers who are ready and willing to ride.

A position had opened up. She was debating on applying for it. If she were hired it would be historic. No other black person had ever served in one of those positions at the time. It was a landmark possibility. She had to do it. I was newly awakened and wanted the same for everyone else. I took out my tool bag and used the best reasoning I had within me.

"You have to do it G," I urged. "It's not just about you. It's about your daughter and other little Black girls here. You have to apply. You can break that ceiling" I said with as much encouragement as I could muster. She listened. She applied and she got the job. I knew she would. She didn't stay in that post for long in the end; because she got another promotion right on its heels.

In many ways Grace saw me better than I was able to see myself. In turn, I saw her better than she was better about to see herself. The thing that was most important was that we were each genuinely concerned for the wellbeing of the other. That is rare. That is powerful. That is necessary- to be a friend at the right time. Being in London stoked my fire.

I spoke for the National Crown Black Prosecutors Association three more times. Liverpool, Nottingham, Birmingham, and Manchester served as cities for the conferences.

Since I knew I would be in town, I searched for some other speaking opportunities. I found some. It didn't come easy. Getting to the venues proved trying.

I was fiercely independent and didn't want any help- that was a big problem at times. Everyone needs help sometimes. I guess pride comes before the fall. The tube was no place for an amateur. The Underground train system in London was more intricate than a spider's web. Guess who got stuck? I had to make sure to "Mind the Gap." There were signs all over the place that displayed that warning. The gap was the space between the platform and the train of about a foot. One misstep could cost you your foot, leg, or life. There was still a gap in me; but it was closing- slowly and surely.

I made a serious mistake. Instead of taking the Underground, I took the trains above ground. I got them mixed up. The train I was on took me way out of the way to reach my location. When I realized my mistake, I got off and headed to the other side of the track. The train came and whisked me back the way I came. The building where I was to speak was about a half mile from the station.

I must have run the whole way. Carrying a video camera and tripod, I must have looked crazy. When I entered the building, sweat was cascading down my face like Niagara Falls. People looked at me like I was in the wrong place. I wasn't. I just looked like I was. When I found my contact, he informed me that I was an hour early. Luckily, I had misread my speaking details.

My time in the UK helped me to understand myself better. It was clear to me and others that I had a gift for speaking. That gift breathed fresh air into me. I needed it badly. My self-esteem and self-confidence grew by leaps and bounds. It felt good. In this I found out a very important thing. Like a car, I had many components and moving parts. One could be broken and the car could still move. I could be up in one area, and down in another. Very rarely is everything going well in every part of a person's life. There was a season for everything. My living arrangements in Detroit had a chilling effect on my time across the pond.

Chapter 20
HOUSE OF HORRORS

"A house divided against itself cannot stand" – Abraham Lincoln

My grandmother had died while I was working at the Wright museum. Her death was a staggering blow for me in many regards. Ruth Alberta was the glue that kept things together. Without her our house started to literally and figuratively fall apart. In her I had lost my greatest champion. My mother and I had lost a superb homemaker.

We lived in a two family flat on Rohns Street. I was nestled upstairs and my mother downstairs. Having suffered with mental illness for about 20 years by the time my grandmother died, Joyce Elaine had not worked in what seemed like an eternity. With her paranoid delusions, I couldn't see that going well. Most importantly, she was not bringing in enough money to maintain a household.

My income from the museum was paltry. Not really knowing the business behind being a public speaker, I only got 3 or 4 well-paying engagements around Black History month. That was not sufficient either. Soon my mother and I were in serious financial trouble. We were on the brink of eviction several times. We had other problems too.

A lack of money meant a lack of utilities. First to go was the water. The landlord was responsible for paying the water bill. Understandably, he only received intermittent rent payments. We really didn't pay him enough to pay the bill. He was a nice guy so he turned it on (illegally) and no one paid the bill.

Next to go was the electricity. We lived in two separate flats. My bright idea was to pay the electricity bill for my mother. I powered the upstairs by a long orange extension cord that I ran out of my mother's kitchen window outside and up through mine. For two years, you could see this orange cord connecting our two kitchen windows.

Moving in together with my mother would have made more sense, but my mother could out-smoke a chimney. The downstairs was always very foggy from her chain smoking. I knew I would die from secondhand smoke in about 15 minutes if I lived downstairs. It was either the long orange extension cord or a Hazmat suit. The extension cord was cheaper.

One of the major drawbacks was the bone-chilling winter temperatures. It gets very cold in Detroit at that time of year. Since I did not have electricity- my furnace did not work. I placed one spare heater in my bedroom that would raise the temperature high enough to sleep comfortably. The problem was the rest of the house would be colder than a freezer. I remember one time it got so cold that the water in the toilet froze.

The other problem was that the pipes would leak and burst. The landlord was slow to fix or replace anything because we rarely paid our rent on time. Because of the leaks, water pressure to the upstairs was so poor that it feebly dribbled out of the faucet. The combination of weak water pressure and below-freezing temperatures made life miserable for me. On one occasion, I had to drop a deuce- but the water in the toilet was frozen. I did it anyway knowing that I would not be able to flush the toilet. Needless to say, my whole house smelled terrible. I had an idea. I thought if I heated up some water in the microwave, I could melt the ice and flush the toilet. It did not work. The smell was magnified ten times by the hot water. My house stank of the essence of Royce for several days until warmer weather came along. After that, I just held it until I got to work to use the restroom. My warm weather problems were just as bad as my cold ones.

Before I left for college, we might see the occasional mouse. After college I do not know if the mice got hooked on steroids or were exposed to gamma radiation; but they now were fully-fledged rats. You could hear them in the walls. It was terrible. Sometimes, it would be so loud that I would wake up from a deep sleep. They looked worse than they sounded.

One scurried across my floor and sent me in to a panic. It was huge. I had no idea that those sounds in the wall were made by those monstrosities. One night after I had just eaten, I fell asleep with my arm hanging over the side of the bed. I was awakened by a burning sensation on one of my fingers. When I looked closely- I saw little teeth marks. I was so angry; I went on the offensive. I vowed to destroy everything with more than two legs in that house. I loaded up on rat poison and conventional traps. What I did worked because I did not hear anymore sounds coming from my walls. The house of horrors made me "sick and tired of being sick and tired." I knew I could do better. I stopped punishing myself and headed back to the shop.

Chapter 21
THE GRIOT PROGRAM, M.ED.

"Education is the most powerful weapon you can use to change the world." – Nelson Mandela

One of my museum teacher buddies at the Wright museum, Hakim Shahid, told us about his goals. He was adamant that he would be a college professor one day. Attaining his doctorate degree was another one of his aspirations. You could see the image that he had in his mind by the way he spoke. For him it was a foregone conclusion. Presently, Dr. Shahid is on faculty at Oakland University in Michigan. He made his vision come true.

Hakim left the museum before I did. He talked about a program at Marygrove College called the Griot Program. It was started to help get more African-American men into the teaching profession. He entered the program and earned his M. Ed. What he did always stuck in my mind. I never forgot it. That's why I try and always surround myself with people that are going somewhere in life.

When it was time, I pulled out that information that I had cataloged in my mind. I was a great public speaker and educational consultant. Even though I was providing enrichment programs in the Detroit Public Schools, training parents for the Detroit Public Schools, and speaking for government agencies- I felt I could do better. This desire came about a few bone-chilling years after my time in the house of horrors.

Marygrove College was a small Catholic school in the middle of Detroit. When I arrived there in 2003, it was in the midst of many improvements. Buildings were being renovated, college sports were being added, and programs were being designed to meet the needs of the community that surrounded it. It was a good place for me to learn how to become a better educator. It was the opportunity on the horizon that I dreamed of when I had my epiphany at the University of Iowa.

My sister Debra had come through Marygrove's hallowed halls years earlier when it was an all-female school. She studied education as well. My sister would go on to become a teacher, administrator, school board member, and superintendent. While I was a student there, she was presented with an outstanding alumni award. Education was in my blood.

The added maturity from life experiences made me an even better student. While at Marygrove I earned only one B. The rest were straight A's. There was a purpose behind my learning that made me hungry for it. It was a great environment for it, too. I did what I did at Iowa and got even better at it. I didn't forget what worked for me, like I did when moving from middle school to Cass Tech and Kettering high school to College. I remembered and applied everything that I needed to. The art of being a student was understood and applied.

I realized that I needed close to complete silence to read. My mind was like an Indy Car. If I hit any small bumps it would crash. Morning times were best for reading. Writing could be done anytime. I was a visual learner. I had to see it to fully comprehend the meaning behind it. My studying area was always well lit. I didn't lounge and study. Things worked best for me whilst sitting at a desk. The most important thing was that I was determined. I would not give up. I would not stop. I would only move for a 5 minute study break every hour. The key was self-discipline. Nothing works without it.

My program was for non-traditional students. Most of my classmates had jobs in education, families, and mortgages. It was a great group of people to learn with and from. Iron sharpens iron. One of my classmates, Nic South, would later hire me to teach middle school English. My buddy Kyle Chandler was instrumental in me getting my first job coaching track at U of D Jesuit High School. Good people can have a positive impact on your life. Keep your circle of friends and associates close, and of a high quality.

Our faculty in the program was phenomenal. They taught in the Sage program that was started to get more African-American women in the teaching program as well. Our faculty had practical experience in teaching K-12 students. Many had been building administrators or central office staff. There was a variety of experience for us to draw from.

Dr. Johnson helped me see myself a little better during class. She had planned for us to work in groups to practice some classroom management strategies. We role-played together. At the end she said that I seemed like I was suffering from a lack of confidence. How correct she was. It takes a good educator to figure out their students so quickly. I didn't even realize that I was giving off certain cues. You can't fix what you can't see.

Dr. Zhiang was our Technology in Education instructor. I learned more about how to use technology in the classroom than I thought was possible. He was the lead instructor for a study abroad program as well. How amazing it would be to visit China I thought. It would be a dream opportunity.

My time at Marygrove strengthened my skills as a speaker, researcher, and writer. My M.Ed. program was just what I needed, right when I needed it. It improved what I did well and identified what I did not. My self-esteem and self-confidence would ebb and flow like the ocean. I was learning though how to think more positively of myself, more often. Like most, when things were not going well, I suffered from low self-esteem and self-confidence.

One of the most important things in my life happened at Marygrove. I learned to self-monitor. Maybe it came from learning how to teach students with different learning styles. Maybe it came from learning how to differentiate instructions. Maybe it was learning to be aware of my biases as an educator. Whatever it was; it helped me in my personal life. I was more aware of myself. Self-awareness was essential for my repairs.

People change because something happens in their mind. They are able to see the need after they see the problem. Tony Robbins said, “Change happens when the pain of staying the same (becomes) greater than the pain of change.” It’s like hitting rock bottom. Only you know when you are there. It takes honesty, courage, and decisiveness. You have to be able to look in the mirror and say to yourself: “It’s your fault.” After that, you can do anything, because you realize that you are in charge of your destiny. You are in charge of your success or failure. It’s totally up to you. Marygrove was one ingredient to this major overhaul. The other was in a house of faith.

Chapter 22

THE TAB

In union there is strength – Aesop

Christian Tabernacle Church, affectionately called the Tab, is located in Southfield, Michigan right outside of Detroit. It would be considered a mega-church. I joined right before I started at Marygrove. My member number was 2539. That wasn't the number of people that attended. That was the number of families. So, if you had 3 people in your family your member numbers would have been 2539-1, 2539-2, and 2539-3. There must have been around 5,000 members when I was their.

It lay on over ten acres of land that included a daycare, elementary school, middle school, family recreation center, and church. There was a full indoor basketball court, arcade games, and pool tables in the recreation center. The campus was well-maintained and stayed clean. A piece of paper knew not to blow across the property.

Dr. James Morman and his wife Loretta Morman held the place together with top notch administrative, management, and financial skills. Using paid staff and volunteers the place ran like an automotive assembly line. Their application of Christian values was the underlying foundation that held the whole ministry together. It was what I needed.

At the time, I was dating a young lady whose mom was a member. We started going to church together. Unfortunately, I butchered the relationship and we broke up. My low self-esteem and self-confidence made long-lasting relationships difficult at best. I seemed to almost intentionally sabotage them. My insecurities were like mountains that few women could climb. I don't blame them. I was hard to love because I was still learning to love myself. No one should have to love you more than you.

I kept going to the church even though I would see her every week. That didn't matter to me. What I was missing was there. A sense of love, belonging, and true friendship permeated every inch of that campus. It started and ended with the pastor- Dr. James Morman.

Every organization fails or succeeds based on its leadership. There is no way around that fact. You don't fire players for bad play during a season, you fire coaches. Dr Morman, lovingly called Shepherd, used excellence and love to change people's lives. Many of his congregation had very little experience with either.

He was a former corporate executive who excelled at his craft. Hard work, attention to detail, and striving for excellence were the keys to his success. He shared much of his former life across the pulpit and in small intimate meetings. We got to know him and he got to know us. He became a father figure to many of us. What worked in his corporate life, he used at the Tab with great success. The church would sometimes attract upwards of 40 new members on Sundays.

There was a host of different ministries for one to volunteer in. Everyone was held to a high standard. Whether you worked in children's church, security, greeter's ministry, music, finance, or the audio/video department- you knew to take your position seriously. You didn't want to get a "fireside" from the pastor. That was short for: fireside chat. It was a personal verbal lashing. No one was exempt. He did it in a loving way. However, no one was looking for that kind of love.

At this time, I really was at a low point. This was before I met Grace and Bruce, and before I traveled around the world as a public speaker and government contractor. Gramps would die shortly thereafter. My hours had been cut in half at the Wright museum. The house of horrors would soon be my living arrangements. I was on a downward spiral.

John Dixon was one of the older brothers in the church who was somewhere in his 50s. He was seeing my girlfriend's mom. We would often see each other over at their house. John was also a close friend to Dr. Morman. Whenever something was going on at the church for the men, he would invite me. I went without my significant other. That was the beginning of repairs for me in several areas.

Many times when the church was having a function, the men would set up and breakdown all the chairs and tables. We did what was necessary. The selfishness that many of us had, that I had, was being washed away. We started thinking about other people besides ourselves. We became servants. I was building on that foundation that was sparked on that bus ride downtown. It's hard to lead if you don't know how to follow.

Shepherd would say over and over, "If we can get the men right, we can get our communities right." We believed him. It was like we were in rehabilitation professionally, psychologically, and spiritually. Men who had been with the church were starting to flourish inside and outside of the church.

Guys were getting promotions and raises at their jobs. Brothers were starting new businesses. Professional athletes were joining the ministry. It became clear- this was a place to get yourself together; whether you were a man or woman. I couldn't wait to get to church and be around these guys. Shepherd often quoted this bible verse, "Iron sharpens iron."

We laughed and joked all the time. It was all good-natured fun. I would be assigned to the security ministry. There were posts around the massive main church building. The most visible were in the front of the sanctuary and at the front exterior doors. At those spots you were going to be seen by the entire congregation at some point. In training for the security ministry- we were warned that women would want to strike up conversations with us. I didn't mind that one bit! We would often have to be "saved" from a sister so we could do our jobs. Later, guys would laugh about who wanted and didn't want to be saved.

When John asked me to come to the church it was initially just to help clean up or set up for functions. I was consistent. It felt good to be there. It felt good to be around a bunch of guys like myself who were getting major and minor repairs done to themselves. Sometimes, I would come in on my own and vacuum bugs out of the light fixtures. Shepherd mentioned that he didn't like that one day. If he didn't like it, I didn't like it. All sons want to please their fathers.

Dr. Morman was one of the most impressive men I had ever met. He had an impeccable taste in clothes. Everyone was influenced by the way he presented himself. He was caring and giving to his congregation. All his good characteristics were transferred down unto us. He had a keen eye. He would often say: "you have to inspect what you expect and expect what you inspect." You couldn't get anything past him.

One day I was working a shift on the security ministry during the week. I was posted outside of his office door. I was sitting reading a book when he entered from the rear outside parking lot. I didn't even see him enter. He asked, "Are you studying for your MBA?" I was thinking "huh?" I was reading a book called "24 Hour MBA". He had seen it in a matter of moments and asked about it immediately. How he saw the cover; I still don't know.

Shepherd asked that a men's choir be formed called Show of Unity. At our first rehearsal we had over 100 men. The music director, Bill Moss, brother of Gospel recording artist, J Moss, had us singing in a 4-part harmony. When they asked for volunteers, I spoke up. I was asked to sing at rehearsal and did a good job. That's something that Dan Charles Green could really do. He was a phenomenal singer.

Singing was easy. Remembering lyrics was my problem. Remembering them in front of 5,000 people was something brand new to me and my memory. The first time I sang my solo, I messed up the words. In an excellent ministry such as this- that wasn't going to fly. Bill Moss was going to make sure of that. He didn't want to get a fireside for putting an unprepared person on stage. I didn't want him to get one either.

I did get an opportunity to sing in front of the church again. Determined to be perfect this time- I focused on the part where I had messed up earlier, and got it right this time. Most things are merely a question of focus. I was pleased with myself. Bill was looking at me sternly; I had no other choice but to deliver the musical goods. That performance inevitably led to another performance.

GRADUATE

A director of several Gospel plays, T.J. Hemphill, was a member of our church. He had produced a play called "Perilous Times" to great success. He was to do a shorter version for our upcoming 8 a.m. and 10 a.m. services on Easter. Costumes, sets, lights, and the whole dramatic production ministry was going to be on display. It was a pretty big deal. I don't think the Tab had done something on such a large scale before with all church members. When there was a call for actors I jumped at the chance.

I landed the role of Jesus. I couldn't mess up the words here. Everyone knew the bible. The church would be packed. Plus it was going to be recorded on video. The stakes were high. Embarrassing myself in front of thousands of people, getting the side-eye from Bill, or a fireside from Shepherd paled in comparison to the consequences of messing up the portrayal of Jesus Christ. I was surely on my way to Hell if I botched this up! I would be the laughing stock of Heaven.

It was an incredible experience. I tried to imagine what it would be like to know the time, place, and manner of your own death. Needless to say, it was extremely depressing, emotional, and draining to take on this portrayal. I did it though, to the best of my abilities. The response was quite amazing.

Shepherd was off to the side- reading passages from the Bible that we were acting out. I remember we were at the part in the story where Jesus was being beaten. The whip actually had some weight to it. It stung a bit. I used that to my dramatic advantage. Every time I was hit I would reach out to the audience that was maybe about 10 feet away. Mrs. Morman and her daughter Loretta were in the front row. They looked horrified. I said to myself, "oh wow this must look real."

Being up on the cross was even more dramatic. Firstly, I was high in the air. The stage was about 3 feet high. There was a rock that served as the stand for the cross that was about 3 feet high. Then, the cross itself was nearly 10 feet talk. I was uncomfortably high in the air, and attempting to act.

You could hear people sobbing all over the sanctuary. It must have been at least 4 or 5 thousand people packed in there for the 10 a.m. service. When I dropped my head as though I had died, I heard a woman yell out: "Oh God!" I then let a long stream of saliva drip out of my mouth that hung off my lip. It glistened in the bright stage limelight. Afterwards someone said to me, "I could see that spit all the way from the back." It seemed my desire to get it right worked out well.

For some time, people from the church would tell me that I had done a good job. One of the guys' son came up to me and said: "That's Jesus daddy!" I thought that was so cute. He couldn't have been more that 4 or 5 years old. The whole experience was a confidence booster.

I really didn't know that I had any acting skills. To do it well in people's opinions was a pretty good feeling. Having Shepherd and T.J. Hemphill trust in me enough to allow me to do it was even more rewarding. There were brothers in the ministry who were helpful to me.

Mark Mayberry had started his own company. It was doing very well. He was a success story. We spoke often about the things I should do to improve things for myself and my still-young public speaking career. I really appreciated his guidance.

Eric Pate was another person I met at the church. He was the cousin of a good friend of mine, Denise, from the University of Iowa. Eric told me about this vendor fair that the Detroit Public School was doing. They were looking for afterschool programming. I went. It was a huge success for me. I would end up providing programs in 5 schools. My bank account needed the assistance.

Shepherd invited guest speakers to the church often. One of my favorites was a pastor from New York named A.R. Bernard. He had been in the Nation of Islam and changed faiths. That was rare. His outlook was rare too. On one visit he said something that I have never forgotten. It was not about "religion" in particular, but life in general. He was speaking about how God wants you to live your best life. He said, "You shouldn't be concerned about the number of hours your work, but added value to each hour you work."

That stuck with me. It made me look at things in a different way. Making $30 in an hour seemed pretty good to me. The idea that I could make more became possible for me. It broke a glass ceiling I had in my mind. Not soon after, Eric approached me with the information about the vendor fair. I was paid over $100 an hour to provide those services. Change has to start in the mind before anywhere else. "If you can believe, all things are possible to him that believes."

My spiritual development at the Tab cannot be understated. I learned some very important things about my faith. The most important was what I was experiencing. In times of difficulty, crisis, and turmoil people need something to hold on to and believe. I knew that God loved me and cared for me. That's why He allowed my steps to be directed to people, and a place that could and did get my life back on track.

Chapter 23

BROTHER IN BEIJING

"The will to win, the desire to succeed, the urge to reach your full potential…these are the keys that will unlock the door to personal excellence." – Confucius

My most anticipated and thrilling attraction on my trip to China was visiting the Great Wall. It is one of the wonders of the modern world. Movies, books, TV, and school had all given me appetizers of what was to come. We were heading to the location that was just a short ride outside of Beijing.

The highway soon turned into road. Peering out of the bus window, I saw a mountain range appearing in the distance. They stretched as far as the eye could see in every direction. I had seen mountains before, but these were different.

I strained to identify a rim on the mountain range. It was almost alien- I had never seen this type of feature before. It stretched out of sight in both directions. Someone broke the silence and anticipation.

"What is that?" one of my travel partners asked.

Suddenly anticipation, excitement, and discovery collided; "That's the Great Wall of China!" someone shouted. My heart beat strong and deep. It was one of the most breathtaking sites I had ever seen.

As we came closer, I was able to pick out more detail. You could see the different watchtower-looking structures all along the wall. I could even make out people moving up and down the stairs. This was a tourist attraction in every sense.

Our bus pulled inside of a parking lot. There must have been 30 to 40 buses lined up in neat rows. People were milling around. The entrance was manned by ticket and money takers. The atmosphere was like one of an amusement park. This attraction happened to be over an astonishing 5,000 miles long.

There were places to eat and buy souvenirs. Picnic tables were filled with people of several different nationalities and ethnicities. It's amazing to hear French, German, English, Chinese, and many other languages being spoken simultaneously at the same place. This was at the base of the stairs.

Several places along the Great Wall there are stairs so that people could get up to the part that lines the mountains. There were a lot of stairs to get to the top. Over 4,000 manmade steps meandered up the mountain side.

The mood started to change the longer we walked up the stairs. Smiles started to fade. Awe waned. Legs started to tremble. Foreheads glistened with sweat. Excitement was traded for exhaustion. The 80 degree heat didn't help.

People were littered up and down the stairs like cars that ran out of gas with their blinkers on. Many looked frustrated, some angry, and others confused. I do not think they realized that doing something worthwhile was going to be so difficult. Such is the story of life. I continued to press upwards and onwards.

Our group members' endurance started to fade. One by one they stopped, rested, and headed back down. Even though there were rest areas along the way, I would not stop. I could not stop. A challenge emerged before me.

Like so many times before, whether by chance, or by my own design, I was confronted with a test. On the surface this seemed like a test of physical endurance. My thighs, calves, and sweat-drenched face confirmed that. It was more than that, though. It was a test of will.

Those who can see the trials and tribulations of life as such usually can succeed at every turn. Those that cannot usually find themselves strewed about like rag dolls on the stairs of life. I found out that there was something that was in me. This something could be summoned, ignited, and set ablaze. Sometimes, it turned on automatically.

The more people I saw heading back down in exhaustion, sitting wearily on the stairs, and giving up, I was more determined to make it to the top. Soon I found myself alone on this journey of will. Such is the story of my life.

At the top was a fortress-like structure. It was made out of stone and looked like a garage. It resembled the structure on English castle walls. It had openings that allowed soldiers to see the approaching enemy hoards. It had a roof top. That is where I went.

I was at the very top. Looking down, I was amazed. The hour climb took me so far up that the buses in the parking lot looked like 9 volt batteries. People looked like ants milling around them. I had traveled a long way up.

GRADUATE

It was so quiet. There were less than 10 people that were there with me. Many of us stared out across the mountain range. A few times a couple of young men let out a yell. It's as though they had to see whether the quietness was real.

It wasn't long before the tears started to flow down my face. The quiet, the difficulty of the climb, and the thoughts of loved ones overwhelmed me. I realized that I was somewhere seeing, doing, and experiencing something that many of my dearest loved ones would not. I wondered why God had allowed me to do so. I stood there, humbled. At that moment, I realized that I could do anything I desired with my life. There would be no limits.

Chapter 24
FEAR AND LOATHING IN BRAZIL

"You drown not by falling into a river, but by staying submerged in it." – Paulo Coelho

The thunderous drums filled the night air of the Pelorinho district of Salvador da Bahia, Brazil. You could hear them pounding like your heartbeat after a quick sprint up a flight of stairs. Their roots were unmistakably African. The slave trade has made an indelible mark on the people and culture. Slave ships first came to Brazil in around 1500. Many were like the ones that had once sailed down the canal next to my Liverpool hotel.

The narrow cobblestone streets were teaming with tourists from all over the world. There were Spanish-designed colonial style buildings that peered down over us like titans. This place was a mix of Europe, Africa, and the New World. That was and is Brazil. Salvador's history was important in understanding its present.

Africans were brought here when the enslavement process of the Native American population failed. They brought with them their gods, food, clothes, and music. Salvador is sometimes called the most African place outside Africa. The word Pelorinho means: "whipping post" in Portuguese. It seems punishment for some still existed there. I saw it with my own eyes.

On our first visit there we were approached by a boy. He looked to be about 8 years old. His hair was matted into dread locks. Soiled clothes hung from a wiry body like that of a scarecrow's. His cocoa brown skin was tanned even darker from the Brazilian sun. He had the look of someone riding a bus in Detroit. His body was alive, but his eyes were dead.

He whipped the coconuts in his tiny hands into motion like a circus clown. When he finished his feverish impromptu performance, he shouted: "Cinco centavos, cinco centavos!" He thought that five Brazilian cents was a good price for his talents. We stood amazed, shocked, and confused. That was our first experience with the whipping post, but not our last.

Pelo was the ghetto, the barrio, the place where the outcasts scrounged for scraps. Many of us from the Hood were cautious, but comfortable there. It was like Rohns Street but with better weather. We weren't afraid of Pelo. Some of our new white Brazilian friends were. I really don't blame them. Anything can happen to a person of too much in a place with people of not enough.

One evening, we headed out to Pelo in three taxis. There were probably 10 or 12 of us. You could see the fear in the eyes of our white Brazilian friends when we stepped out of the cab into the night. As we walked through the streets, I served as part sentry, part secret service. I repeated "nao obrigado" to the beggars sternly, looking deep into their eyes. They understood that 'no thank you' meant 'no thank you'. I just wanted to make sure that everyone was okay. It was a reasonable service I provided.

I wanted the fearful to have a nice time in their city. It was hard for me to see anyone curled up on a Cambus in any part of the world. It was the least I could do for admiring their women so keenly. The poor leaked out of Pelo like oil from a cracked gasket. They were everywhere. You could see the crushing poverty; day or night.

My walk to ACBEU every morning was uneventful, but eye-opening. From my apartment in the Port of Barra, overlooking the Atlantic Ocean, I would walk by people who made Cinco Centavos look like Richie Rich. Their brown and black skin made us familiar. We were kin. I knew what it was like to struggle. I knew what it was like to not have enough.

Just outside the gates of my apartment building, homeless people slept. They huddled outside together in the nooks and crannies of buildings on the ground like discarded pieces of paper. Walking by neither startled or woke them. They were in a sunken place. It was common to see dogs lying with them on their cardboard beds. Their misery was shared with man's best friend. It was difficult to tell who was doing better in the partnership.

My heart sunk the morning I saw a pile of dirty tattered clothes raise like the dead to show a woman that greatly resembled my deceased grandmother, Ruth Alberta. Her leathery skin was creased and weathered by the forces of age and the outdoors. Grey hair encased her head like barbed wire. Any desire to help her was nullified by the bewildering fact that she was only one of the 20 or 30 people in this condition that I would see on my 20 minute walk. As saddening as her image was; there is still another I have burned into my memory.

On one particular corner lived a family. I don't mean they lived in the corner house or apartment, but they literally took up residence on the corner. Walking by them every day for 6 weeks; their story was written in my imagination.

They seemed different than the other homeless. They had possessions. Many of them were stacked and lined neatly off the corner, down the side street. I could see clothes, cooking equipment, and some toiletries. It was like they had just been evicted. They hadn't yet trickled down to the bare-bone rock bottom of Brazilian poverty. They didn't have a cart with all their possessions. They still held on to their dignity. They had as much as you can have whilst living on the street.

Even though other homeless people were with someone else, they didn't seem connected. It was like they were forced together by unforeseen circumstances. Like unwilling participants of some cruel experiment, forced to co-exist. The family on the corner was different because they seemed like a unit. They seemed to be pieces to the same puzzle that they refused to let go. It's like they realized that all we have is one another.

There was a man, woman, and small girl. She looked to be around 6 or 7 years old. Strangely, when I saw her, my mind asked the question: "Why isn't she in school?" It was like my mind was blocking out the fact that she was destitute. That she was a castaway on dry land. School was the least of her problems. Rain, the searing heat, the elements, and food to cook on her family's outdoor gas burner were much more important to her in these trying times.

They were there, no matter rain or shine. The torrential flash rain showers did nothing to wash them away from their location. Sometimes they would be milling around, lounging, or just staring blankly at the people passing by. I don't remember them ever asking for any money. Existence was enough until it wasn't, I guess. That wasn't the most amazing part, though.

People did not see them. They didn't see them like I saw them. They didn't see them like my group members from the US saw them. I watched as people walked by, around, and sometimes, over them. Most Brazilians saw them as a nuisance. Not like the "don't ask me for change" type of nuisance; but like a crack in the sidewalk type of nuisance. Their humanity seemed to be lost on most. They were merely a walking hazard like a puddle of water to step over. There were many Brazilians who were concerned with the hardship of their countrymen and women; but I didn't see them on that corner. The McDonalds right around the corner told the tale of the other story I uncovered in Salvador.

McDonalds was McDonalds. Big Macs, Quarter Pounders, fries were all on the menu. How could it mean anything else? It was a hangout during certain parts of the evening and night. The cool people hung out here. That's nothing new. You had to really look close at the clientele. The "cinco centavos" crowd was absent.

The crowd was lighter in complexion and much more affluent. You could tell that these people had money. Their clothes were nicer, cleaner, and matching. Hair was neat, cut, and styled. Little girls' dresses were pressed, prim, and proper. These folks didn't sleep on cardboard. They slept on beds that were made up by maids.

Outside, Honda Civics and Accords glistened in the Brazilian sun. Guys with their hats turned to the back wiped, posed, and chatted. When I found out that these foreign cars sold for 70K, I started to understand. McDonalds here was for the upper middle class. It was the meeting place for the visible and not the invisible.

The prices on the menu were not high for us, the Americans. But for the average Brazilian, living on about $3,000 American dollars a year, eating at McDonalds was a stretch on the resources. A Third World Country defined itself right before our eyes. I didn't have to look far to see it play out at the home of my host family.

My room overlooked the Atlantic Ocean and the Bay of All Saints. Barra beach was right on the other side of the street. I would be awakened every morning by the sounds of waves slapping against the rocks. It was fantastic. I spent many evenings watching the sunset from my bedroom window. My host family was a kind, blue-collar, and gritty type.

The dad was a retired military man. We talked politics. He was a down to earth, matter of fact, honest kind of guy; imagine General Patton in a Speedo. One night when I was feeling sick, he gave me this tiny little pill. In less than 5 minutes, I had puked up my stomach and was feeling better. He got results.

His wife was his perfect match. She was simple, caring, and dependable. When she cooked, your stomach listened. Her and my grandmother must have gone to the same cooking school. Lunch was the biggest meal of the day routinely in Brazil. It was lavish. Upwards of 10 courses would put me right to sleep afterwards. Her homemade ice cream was the best. She was a very sweet woman.

Their two sons were different in that younger/ older brother type of way. The older one was taking life as it came. The younger brother was the go-getter. He spoke 4 different languages and was in law school. He was the type of guy who would be executive of something in very little time. His crystal blue eyes charmed the ladies into submission.

The housekeeper was the most interesting of them all. She very rarely spoke. She looked younger than me. Walking around the house barefoot, she cleaned, washed, and straightened like she was one demotion from a cardboard bed. I was amazed that she would wash my underwear by hand. I wouldn't even do that.

One day at dinner time, the dad and I had our most revealing conversation. We were talking about the favelas, Brazilian ghettos. He talked about how they were dangerous. One could even hear gunshots ringing out in the streets he mentioned. I didn't want to tell him about Rohns Street. He didn't know he had someone from an American favela sleeping under his roof. My Prada loafers and Movado watch kept my secret hidden very well.

We got on the subject of salaries and wages for housekeepers. Everyone had a maid in Brazil. At least all of the places where our group members stayed had them. He was surprised to learn that I didn't have a maid. I explained that you really had to be wealthy in America to have one. He never said it explicitly, but he talked about how the domestics worked just for food. I concluded that our cocoa complexioned housekeeper was closer to that cardboard bed than I had imagined.

Clara's personality was a mix of used car salesman, movie star, and CEO. Her neon bright smile, humor, and warmth were just what ACBEU (in Portuguese it means cultural association for Brazil and the United States) needed to be successful. Their racket was language. It was a great business too. Everyone outside of the United States understood that English was the language of access, money, and opportunity.

Brazilians were keenly aware of that fact. Clara knew how to capitalize on that understanding. She could sell an Eskimo a bikini in a snow storm.

Besides teaching Brazilians English, it taught mostly American college students Portuguese. That probably made the most money. Tuition, room, and board were easily north of $4,000. The average yearly salary for a Brazilian was easily south of $4,000. There were around 70 to 80 American students at any given time during the year. The classes lasted from 6 weeks to 3 months. We probably looked like fat little piggy banks walking through those hallways.

The school was gated. Where we lived was gated. Everything was gated. It was truly amazing to see armed guards at every gated apartment. Sometimes, apartments had 2 guard stations. ACBEU had a guard that greeted us with a "Bom Dia" every morning. He was there to protect the profits. When people are living right on the corner there was a need for gates and guns. Hungry desperate people can get quite ornery.

In the afternoons, school-age students would take our place in the classrooms. They were not the children who juggled fruit for money. Nor were they the kind of kids that people stepped over in the streets. They were well to do. They were the private school, nanny type of kids. You didn't have to ask them, you could tell by the way they carried themselves. You could tell by the way they took over the school, ran the hallways, and yelled at the top of their lungs. Privilege was their plaything. All rich Brazilians were not bratty.

Riding buses in Salvador was as confusing as navigating a maze. It took me a long time to figure that out. Taking the 10 minute bus ride up the hill to ACBEU was easy. Try to take it anywhere else was harrowing.

I had just left the mall and didn't feel like walking the 15 minutes back home. There was a row of bus stops near the entrance. I was sure one of them would take me near home. Fear was my first mistake. Fear of rejection was my biggest problem. I was afraid to unleash my hellish dialect of Portuguese and ask for help. I just picked a bus, paid the fare, and got on. Making decisions based on fear rarely works out well.

Things got off to a bad start because people were just finishing work. The bus was packed. I had a guy jammed up so close to me it felt like I was wearing one of Pele's sweaty soccer jerseys. His hot breath on the back of my neck made me feel like I was in an oven. The dripping wet bus windows obscured my view.

As the bus emptied, the windows dried, and I realized that I did not recognize any of the scenery flying by. I was gripped by fear. Maybe if I wait, I thought, things would get better. They didn't. I was using my American mindset to figure out a Brazilian problem.

In the states, buses usually did one route and then turned around and travelled in the opposite direction. These buses would do several different routes at one time. The driver changed the sign on the front of the bus several times before I figured this out. By that time it was too late. I was well and truly lost.

The scenery had changed from city, to country, to "where the Hell am I?" very quickly. My apartment building sat right on the Bay of All Saints. It and the city were a faint twinkle in the darkness of the night. I had been on the bus for over an hour and was at least 30 miles from home. I had to do something.

I decided to get off the bus. It had to be a good spot, I thought. I wanted to make sure a bus stop was right on the other side of the street. Additionally, I wanted to make sure someone was standing there. I didn't want to be alone, in the dark, and lost. The moment of truth came. I was forced to take a leap of faith.

I rang the bell and got off the bus. Stepping down into the dark unknown was telling. Immediately something turned on. I wish I knew what it was, what it is. It is that something that says: "you have to get this right; right now... there are no other options for you." It is the something that says there is no room for error. I was a continent away from friends and family, and 30 miles away from anyone who knew me.

Casually, I walked across the street like I had done it a million times. There was a street merchant at the bus stop selling his wares. "Quanto est Skol?", I asked him in decent Portuguese. I handed him the money, he handed me the beer. I sipped it while I leaned on a sign by the bus stop. I allowed two buses to pass before I recognized the destination on the front.

I asked the money taker was the bus going near the Port of Barra, where I lived. He said yes. I understood him and he understood me. The faint twinkle of lights started to become the city I had known for over a month. Streets, buildings, and features of the city became familiar again. I had made it back.

I learned a lot about myself. Bus rides were my incubator for self-reflection. If allowed, fear can paralyze a person. It can stop them from moving, progressing, and achieving. It is the enemy of anything good in a person's life.

It usually comes in three distinct ways. Fear of rejection is when a person is afraid of not being accepted by people. People who have been abandoned in some way usually struggle with this one. Fear of loss is when a person believes that their actions will cause them to lose something or someone close to them. But as they say- nothing wagered nothing gained. On Rohns Street they would say "scared money don't make money". The last was fear of failure. Many people don't start many things because they are afraid of failing. The truly successful have literally failed themselves to success. Thomas Edison said he never failed once; but found out 10,000 ways that something didn't work.

Additionally, I learned that the problems that we get into- we usually cause ourselves. Sometimes, we are our biggest enemies. The devil didn't make us do it. We made us do it. I put myself in a serious predicament because I was initially afraid to ask for help. What makes that situation even more unbelievable is that I knew I had a working cell phone in my pocket the whole time.

Chapter 25

MARSHALL, U OF D, DPA, AND THE STUDENT MECHANIC

"It is easier to build strong children than to repair broken men" – Frederick Douglass

My first teaching job was at a charter middle school in one of the poorest and most violent parts of Detroit. The Herman Garden housing project had just been demolished, but it dispersed its unsavory occupants into the surrounding neighborhood. Those children populated my school and the middle school right across the street.

My school, Detroit Premier Academy, often called DA, was the low octane version of Mae C. Jemison middle school. It was a Detroit public school. A former co-worker of mine at DPA said the first time he drove to work, he saw kids hanging from the second story windows of Jemison. I'm not sure if they were trying to get in or get out. Either way, those kids were built for speed.

If you were expelled from DPA, you just went 200 feet over to Jemison. One such student was awarded several stitches in the head after one of her new classmates hit her with a combination lock. Another student got her folders flushed down the toilet. The welcoming committee was quite fond of giving DPA students the full service. Jemison was like Rohns Street on steroids. DPA students had problems too.

One of my students was commonly pawned off to her drug-addicted mother's boyfriends to provide sexual favors for money. Another one of my students' mother was dying of cancer while she was in jail. The heart-breaking stories go on and on. It's needless to say that my students needed someone who cared about them. It was a stark difference from where I had done my student teaching just a few months earlier.

The University of Detroit Jesuit High School and Academy was a 15 minute car ride from DPA. The students drove better cars than the staff. Their parents paid a pretty penny to have their kids go to one of the most prestigious prep schools in the Detroit area. They were the navy blazer and khaki pants crowd. Kids graduated and went to the Armed Forces Academies and Ivy League schools. Your back up school was the University of Michigan, which is one of America's best public institutions.

As different as both schools were, they shared something in common. Many of the African-American boys were in search for a idea of Black masculinity. Even those at U of D that came from two family households seemed to be confused. They had a male role-model in the house, usually a very good one. Yet, they still stumbled down their paths. Some would be expelled and have to go to schools like Cass Tech.

The same popular culture that fueled Rohns Street, Herman Gardens, seemed to do the same for U of D. These corrosive images went up and down the social economic ladder with the same results. Kids that had a daddy in the house usually only dabbled in this search. They were more likely to get straightened out if they veered off course. For some of them it was more like a hobby. When they used the f-word they were sure to pronounce the "er" at the end.

Boys with less direction sagged their pants and were disruptive in class. Some of them never graduated from U of D. They lost out on a phenomenal opportunity to get a great high school education and prepare for the difficulty of university coursework. U of D was the kind of school I needed. Kyle Chandler and I tried to help as much as possible.

Kyle was teaching at the U of D, finishing up his master's in the Griot program at Marygrove, and coaching his younger brother who attended the school in track. Being a graduate of U of D, he knew the pitfalls that Black boys could experience. He worked hard to make sure his younger brother, Mike, avoided them. I followed his lead and took as many boys under my wing as possible. I had suddenly become the mentor, after living all these years as the mentee.

Jarius was one of those kids that had the potential to be president of anything, anywhere, and at any time. He was one of the most charismatic boys I had ever met at U of D. He could talk his way out of anything with a devilish grin. Imagine a 16 year old Black version of Bill Clinton from Detroit. That was him. Charisma can take you a long way if you use it right. Jarius didn't always use it in the best way.

It seems that Jarius used his superpowers for evil more times than for good. Teachers disliked the classroom disruptions. He had to serve many stints in detention. Finally, he was put on disciplinary probation, and then expelled. There aren't many bad kids. Just like Jarius, they simply need direction. He lived with his grandmother, with no parents in site.

We went to a college bowl football game at Ford Field, the home of the Detroit Lions. His grandmother was happy that someone showed they cared. She knew that a positive male figure in his life was important. I talked to him. He heard me. We kept in contact for many years. I really hope that something I said or did help him until he met his next GK and James Lee.

DPA was a different environment. There were only a few boys in the 8th grade that had fathers present in their lives. That was the same for the rest of the middle school. Fathers just simply weren't present. One of my teaching mentors, Leon Reed Jr. and Reg Lane started a group called Distinguished Gentleman. It was a mentoring group for boys. Principal Vondra Glass allowed it to happen. He knew the power of mentorship. We couldn't save them all, but we certainly could try.

Marshall was good-looking dark-skinned kid in one of my classes. Just like most, he was being raised by a single mother. The love she had for her son was clear. The ability to have a positive male figure around was out of her reach. By the time I met Marshall, he had been held back twice. That is an indication of trouble to come. He tried, but he wasn't a good student. His behavior was great. We adults couldn't find the right motivation or learning strategy that could have helped Marshall.

He did get his grades up enough during basketball season to play in a few games. Talent on the basketball court was something he did have. He could play very well. Many kids could. But sports can only help those who can get the job done in the classroom. That wasn't Marshall.

I remember pulling him out of class many times to talk to him about being a leader. He didn't relish that role. His self-esteem was low; it seemed familiar. When I looked at him it was like I was looking at myself in the mirror. I knew that his life could go either way. He was at the crossroads. We were happy that he was able to graduate from middle school. Unfortunately, high school was a different matter.

He moved to high school and I moved to another teaching job. We lost track of each other. When I saw one of my old students from DPA I would ask about him. He wasn't going to school regularly. That was a bad sign. There are only two things for black boys to get into: school or trouble.

The details were sketchy. They always are about these types of things. Marshall was going somewhere at night. I don't know who he was with and I don't know what he was doing. I just know that he was shot and killed. That was it. The story of Marshall.

When I heard the news I was struck with an overwhelming feeling of guilt. I felt that I had let him down. He was in my class. I saw him every day. Why couldn't I have said or done something to change the course of his short life? I came to learn that it wasn't my fault. It wasn't his teachers or staff at the school's fault either. We did our best. We cared.

I learned that there was a razor thin line between Marshall and I. Sitting under our dining room table on New Year's Eve 30 years earlier and I could have very easily been Marshall. My brief attempt to get into Detroit's dangerous dope game could have seen me being him. Those two times around the Warehouse night club and I could have been him. Walking down a deserted Iowa City street after a night of drinking and I could have been Marshall. Trust and believe there are many more times not discussed in this book where I could have been senselessly killed like Marshall.

Since the stakes can be high for the young people I come into contact; I seek to maximize the time I spend with them.

Every moment is a teachable one. I try and give them a diagnostic to see what traits they have that may give them trouble. Like a mechanic, I try to fix the problem, motivate, and inspire them along the way. It's a labor of love, of hope, and of charity. I try to do for them what I needed someone to do for me: care. This is my life as the Student Mechanic.

Chapter 26

CONCLUSION, THE CLIFF NOTES

"We must let go of the life we have planned, so as to accept the one that is waiting for us." - Joseph Campbell

What I have to say is so important, I want to make it as clear as possible. I know that these words can drastically change your life. So, here is the abridged version:

1. **Where you come from doesn't have to stop you.** The culture of the place we come from guides, impacts us, and influences us. However, it does not have to determine where we end up. **Students:** There are statistics and research to suggest that social economic status does influence a person's academic outcomes. Nevertheless, you can decide to be something different by learning and developing good study stills, goal-setting, working hard, and never giving up. **Professionals:** Your keys to success are similar to that of the student. You must become something new in order to achieve something different

than your hometown usually produces. It's up to you to goal-set, challenge yourself, and never let anything stop you- not even yourself.

2. **Who your family is doesn't have to be an obstacle.** Just like where we were raised; we don't have to let our family influence our success. Sometimes, family can be impediments to our upward mobility. There are many reasons for this. None of them can be your concern. **Students:** Your success in school is not due to anything besides hard work, the development of sound study habits, perseverance, time management, people management, and money management. **Professionals:** When you accept the fact that no one owes you anything- especially your family- you can be more focused on your success. It is a question of personal development, painstaking hard work, determination, and planning.
3. **Self-Discipline is the key for your success.** Students and professionals, you must decide to do what is necessary, for as long as is necessary, to see your desired result. It is that simple.
4. **Persistence and Perseverance will determine the level of your success.** Thomas Edison once said: "I have not failed. I've just found 10,000 ways that something won't work." You have to be willing to endure the issues and problems that are sure to come at the least convenient time. Push past them and success is possible.
5. **You can never stop learning.** Students and professionals you must realize that your lives are largely based on what you know. So, you must be committed to learning for the rest of your life. What you need to be successful is not

hidden. It is not a secret. You can learn your way to success.

6. **Your circle of friends and associates should help you.** If you are not learning from those around you, being challenged, hearing constructive criticism, and being mentored- you need to start deleting people immediately. There is a difference in being an aid to someone and being drained by someone. I heard that we make within $5,000 to our 5 closest friends and associates. This is telling. Sit at the feet of giants and learn.
7. **Givers will always get.** You can call it karma or whatever you like. There is a law in this universe. What you put out will always come back. Knowing that, you must think, speak, and do what you want for yourself. You must be an answer to problems. Down the line answers will be provided for you. Money helps, but it doesn't solve every problem.
8. **Stop thinking small.** You must dare to think big. Your goals must be large. Don't be afraid to do what has never been done. Les Brown said: "Shoot for the moon, because if you miss, you'll land in the stars."
9. **Fear is a liar and a thief.** You will never live your best life if you allow fear to guide your thoughts and actions. Fear of loss, rejection, and failure are insidious. They can make you lie to yourself if you allow them. You must be honest with yourself. Will Smith said in his early career that he would force himself to do things that made him afraid. I heard a quote once that said: "Do the thing you fear and the death of fear is certain." You must be brave.
10. **Believe in something bigger than yourself.** You can call it the Supreme Being or any of the many other names we

humans have decided to use. I believe in Jesus Christ. In times of distress in your life it is extremely useful to be able to look to a higher power. Faith and belief is an essential component to success. I always believed that my high power was working in conjunction with my efforts. When I had no answers, I had faith that my God would come to my rescue. In every one of those times; that was the case.

The most important thing I have learned is that there is no secret to success. Everything that a person needs to know can be learned. The examples are all around us. Successful people share many of the same traits and behaviors as each other.

The other thing I learned is that during the course of my life when things were going well, I was exhibiting certain behaviors. When things were going bad, I was not. I was in total control. When I came to that realization, taking responsibility for my actions, I was then able to create success out of nothing.

It did not matter whether I was 6 or 36, in elementary school or college, the same recipe worked. The process is timeless and doesn't hinge on race, creed, color, religion, or sexual orientation. You may be faced with different obstacles, but success is possible for everyone. Success at any level is determined by the development of learnable skills and behaviors. That knowledge will ensure that you continue to **GRADUATE.**

Resources

Davis, Michael W.R. and Wagner, James. Ford Dynasty: A Photographic History. Arcadia Publishing. Mt. Pleasant, SC. 2002.

Williams, Jeremy. Detroit: The Black Bottom Community. Arcadia Publishing. Mt. Pleasant, SC. 2009

Wilson, William Julius. When Jobs Disappear: The World of the New Urban Poor. Knopf Doubleday Publishing Group, New York, NY. 1997.